Forgotten Heroes
Irish Casualties in the North Russian
Intervention 1918 – 1919

Pat Twomey

ORLA
KELLY
PUBLISHING

Table of Contents

Acknowledgements

My family inspires me in everything I do, and I thank them for supporting me in my endeavours. In particular, I want to thank my partner, Bernie, for her patience and understanding during the long hours spent on this work. To my children, Michelle, Patrick, Kieran, and Claire, you inspire and make me proud every day of my life.

While researching this project, my comrades at the Great War Forum were most helpful. They generously provided key nuggets of information that were invaluable in bringing this work to fruition. In particular, I would like to thank my friend Damian Wright, a world-renowned expert on the 'Russian Intervention', who has been more than willing to share his vast knowledge with me and promptly responded to my many queries over the last twenty years.

I would also like to thank (in no particular order) the following people, without whose help this book would not have been possible: Alexei Suhanovsky, Mike Grobbel, Richard R. Pyves, Al Richardson, Steven Kelly, Yvonne Kennedy, Gordon Rae, Patrick Groom, Gordon Pennell and Alan Curragh.

Thanks to the organisations and institutions that allowed me to use their photos. If I've forgotten anyone, my sincere apologies.

Introduction

The Great War

The assassination of Archduke Franz Ferdinand on 28th June 1914 by a Bosnian Serb provided the spark that lit the fuse in what would become known as the Great War between the Central Powers (mainly Germany, Austria-Hungary, the Ottoman Empire, and Bulgaria from 1915) and the Entente Powers or Allies (primarily the United Kingdom, France, Russia, Italy, Japan, and the US from 1917). The introduction of new weapons, improvements in defensive positions, and the balance of forces between the two sides prevented either one from gaining a quick victory. Germany's first objective was to march through Belgium, defeat France, and then concentrate on the Eastern Front against Russia. Following the invasion of Belgium, the Germans soon became bogged down on the Belgium/French border as the Allies eventually halted the German advance around the Marne River valley. A counter-offensive by the Franco/British forces saw the Germans retreat as far as the Aisne River, and both armies attempted to outflank each other's northern flank in what became known as the 'race for the sea'.

With neither side able to outflank the other the 'race' finally ends at the North Sea coast of Belgium in mid-October 1914. Both armies began digging trenches to hold the line and plan for further advances. The continuous line of trenches from the North Sea to Switzerland became the focus of offensives and counter-offensives for the next four years in what became known as the Western Front.

While the Western Front was experiencing a 'stalemate' in operations, the Eastern Front was much more fluid as the war developed there. The principal belligerents on the Eastern Front were the Russians and Romanians on the side of the Allies, while the Germans, Austro-

Hungarians and eventually (October 1915) the Bulgarians sided with the Central Powers. The line of the Eastern Front was twice as long as the Western Front as it stretched from the Baltic Sea in the north to the Black Sea in the south. In August 1914, the Russian army attempted to invade Germany. Initially, it seemed to succeed, but the Germans eventually counter-attacked. In the Battle of Tannenberg, the Russians suffered a humiliating defeat with estimated losses of 90,000 dead, injured or taken prisoner.[1] The main weakness of the Russians was their inability to equip their massive army with sufficient artillery shells, motorised vehicles, and boots.[2] To overcome these weaknesses, the Allies transported supplies and munitions to Russia through the far northern port of Archangel. However, as Archangel was frozen solid during winter, the port of Murmansk (ice-free all year round) was chosen as a staging post. The construction of a rail line from Murmansk to Archangel was begun in 1915 to transport the above supplies.

In early October 1915, the Allies opened another front against the Central powers when they landed a small force of British and French troops in Salonika to support Serbia and deter Bulgaria from participating in the war. Many of the troops assembled for the 'Salonika Front' had just taken part in the failed Gallipoli campaign, which attempted to knock Turkey out of the war, and were war-weary and tired from that campaign. The day after the Allies landed in Salonika, the Central Powers attacked Serbia, and a week later, Bulgaria joined in the attack. While the Salonika front, also known as the Macedonian front, came too late to save Serbia, it did, eventually, create a stable front running from the Adriatic Sea (in Northern Albania) to where the river Struma enters the Aegean Sea. This front was to remain stable until September 1918, when the Allied offensive resulted in Bulgaria's surrender and Serbia's liberation. Two months later, at 11.00 am on the 11th of November, 1918, the armistice was signed between the Entente and their opponents, Germany, which saw an end to hostilities.

Ireland and the Great War

When war broke out in Europe in 1914, the political situation in Ireland was complex, to say the least. Being part of the United Kingdom for several centuries, Ireland was bitterly divided between those (Nationalists) agitating for Home Rule and independence and those (Unionists) wishing to remain part of the British empire. When, in 1913, the home rulers seemed to be gaining momentum for a devolved government, the northern Unionists formed a paramilitary organisation known as the Ulster Volunteer Force (UVF), and shortly after, the Nationalists formed the Irish Volunteer Force (IVF).

By the summer of 1914, the Home-rulers had won the right to limited self-government in Parliament. This alarmed the Unionists, who now flocked to join the UVF to 'defend the union'. Many believed at this time that a civil war was inevitable in Ireland, and both paramilitary groups, the UVF and IVF, were actively preparing for that eventuality.

When Britain declared war on Germany at the beginning of August 1914, the promise made to Ireland contained within the Government of Ireland Act 1914 (also known as the Home Rule Bill) was postponed as the focus was now on the war in Europe. Surprisingly, both Unionists and Nationalists decided to support the British war effort, and many of the UVF and IVF volunteers enlisted in the British army. In the first six months of the war, more than 50,000 Irishmen answered the call and enlisted in the British army.[3] While some joined for ideological reasons, perceiving the plight of small nations such as Belgium and Serbia as similar to Ireland's predicament, others joined for economic reasons, and others for a sense of adventure. Seventeen-year-old Cork man Tom Barry, who would go on to fight with the IRA in Ireland's war of independence, claimed that he joined for no other reason 'than that I wanted to see what the war was like, to get a gun, to see new countries and to feel a grown man'.[4] However, as Irish casualties increased during the war years and the political situation altered in Ireland, many turned against the war, and the recruitment numbers in Ireland slowed significantly. The Easter Rising in 1916 saw nationalists take over the centre of Dublin and declare Ireland a 'Republic'. While this action was not wholly supported by the majority of people in Dublin or Ireland, the execution of the leaders, following the suppression of the rising, was not received well by the Irish public, and this helped to garner broader support for the republican cause. Soldiers returning from the frontlines of the Great War at this time were experiencing a significantly different political environment than the one they had left a short few years previously.

Northern Russia

When the guns fell silent on the Western Front on the 11th hour of the 11th day of the 11th month in 1918, many people heaved a sigh of relief that the long-running Great War was finally over. In the previous four years, it is estimated that over 40 million casualties had occurred, including 20 million dead and 21 million injured.[5] A number of those were from Ireland, and the number of Irish-born soldiers killed in action in World War 1 has been estimated to be between 40,000 [6] and 49,000,[7] the most recent research,[8] estimates that over 31,000 were from the Republic of Ireland alone and another 14,000 from Northern Ireland, which gives a total of 45,000 Irishmen who perished in the Great War.

But while peace had finally broken out on the Western Front, hostilities continued in many parts of the world. In North Russia, just as the Armistice came into force, a fierce battle occurred on the banks of the River Dvina between Allied forces and the Red Army. The intervention by Allied troops in Russia began following the 1917 October Revolution, which saw the communists, under Vladimir Lenin, take control of Russia from the Provisional Government that had ousted the Tsarist regime. Five months after taking control, on 3rd March 1918, the Communists signed a treaty (Brest-Litovsk) with Germany that ended the war on the Eastern Front. This development alarmed the Allies as they feared the redeployment of German troops to the Western Front might overwhelm the seriously depleted British and French armies. Even more alarming was that the

Allies had been using the ports of Murmansk and Archangel, in North Russia, as bases for stockpiling military equipment to support the Eastern Front and thus reduce pressure on the front at France and Flanders. When the Bolsheviks decided to make peace with Germany, the Allies now feared that the vast amount of military equipment in the ports of Murmansk and Archangel would fall into the hands of their enemy. To safeguard this equipment, but under the guise of helping and supporting the local Soviet, a landing party of 130 Royal Marines disembarked in Murmansk on 6th March 1918 and began to settle in and await further orders.

The British began a campaign to persuade their allies of the urgency of the situation in North Russia and the need to intervene. Over the next couple of months, the British succeeded, as by June 1918, the Allied Supreme War Council, at their meeting in Versailles, agreed on the scale and objectives of the operation. The campaign's main aim was to re-establish the Eastern Front; other objectives were to secure the military stockpiles in Murmansk and Archangel and support the anti-German factions in Russia. One element in this faction was the Czechoslovak Legion, making its way along the Trans-Siberian Railway to Vladivostok to be transported to the Western Front to continue their war against the Germans.[9]

A more ambitious objective of the intervention was Winston Churchill's plan to defeat the Bolsheviks and end communist rule in Russia. He claimed that 'of all the tyrannies in history, the Bolshevist tyranny is the worst, the most destructive, and the most degrading'.[10] He planned to join up the disparate anti-Bolshevik forces in Russia, including the Czechoslovak Legion, and 'strangle Bolshevism in its cradle'.[11] The following month (July 1918), following a request by Britain and France, the United States President, Woodrow Wilson, reluctantly agreed to send a limited number of American soldiers to help in the campaign.

It was agreed that the Allies would send up to eight battalions to North Russia, mainly British, American, Canadian, and French forces, and would be placed under British Military command.[12] A number of these troops that found themselves in North Russia were Irish, and by the time the last troops left North Russia in September 1919, twenty-one of these Irish-born soldiers were killed or died in the frozen wastes of this inhospitable land – the following provides a background to these forgotten Irish-born soldiers who gave their lives in a war that they must have found difficult to understand.

This is their story.

Chapter 1

Background

The intervention in North Russia began with the landing of 130 Royal Marines in Murmansk in March 1918 to safeguard the war supplies that had been landed there in the previous number of months. Two months later, the US cruiser *Olympia* arrived in Murmansk to support the interventionist aims of the Allies. Following skirmishes between Red Finns and White Finns across the Murmansk/Finnish border, the soviet leader in Murmansk, Alexei Yuryev, fearful of a White Finnish invasion, requested help from the British to deter the Finns from invading across the Kola Inlet. Because the British feared that the White Finns would supply the Germans with a base in the Kola Peninsula for their submarines, they agreed to the request. They dispatched forty Marines and 40 Red Guards to Kandalaksha near the Finnish border. Armed with Lewis guns and supported by a Naval 12-pounder, this force quickly established control of the area and ensured the Finns retreated across the border. Despite the successful cooperation between the Murmansk Soviet and the British troops, the leaders in Moscow were not happy and, under pressure from Germany, sent a series of telegrams to Murmansk, ordering them to stop accepting help from the British. The head of the Soviet Government, Vladimir Lenin, telegraphed the Murmansk Soviet, claiming that England's direct objective was in '...overthrowing the Workman's and Peasants' power', but the Murmansk Soviet continued to collaborate with the Allies and negotiated a formal agreement signed by both parties in July 1918.[13]

American sailors from the USS Olympia in Murmansk, Russia, July 1918 (NHHC)

The British and their allies now turned their sights on Archangel. Alarmed at the prospect of the Germans getting their hands on the armaments stockpiled there, they began to build up their forces in Murmansk to invade Archangel. As stated, Archangel had become the primary location for delivering Allied war supplies. By mid-1918, millions of pounds worth of armaments lay stockpiled on the docks and warehouses of that port. The War Office was determined not to let the sizeable military stockpile fall into unfriendly hands and set about securing the port.

Following a staged coup by some 'White Russians' against the Soviet government in Archangel, Allied warships, led by Adventure Class cruiser HMS *Attentive*, sailed into the port of Archangel where General Poole declared Martial Law and, in effect, took over the running of the city and surrounding area. The allied troops consisted mainly of British and a small number of American sailors from USS *Olympia* who were under the command of Poole. The main thoroughfares south of Archangel were the railroad and the Dvina River, the routes the communists in charge of Archangel took as they fled the city. Consequently, the first objective of the Allies was to secure these routes as far south as possible to deal with the counter-offensive that was sure to come from the Bolshevik troops who had vacated the city and who would be joined by battalions of the Red Army who would rush to Archangel to challenge the 'foreign imperialist invaders'.

The Allies also set about reinforcing their troops on the ground so that they could confront the Red Army and achieve the objectives of the Intervention. The British sent a flotilla of over 20 ships, including two seaplane carriers, and battalions from the Royal Marine Light Infantry, Royal Scots, Royal Engineers, Royal Army Medical Corps, and several other battalions to try and hold back the Red Army who were determined to expel them. The US forces, known as the Polar Bear Expedition, consisted of around 5,000 troops drawn mainly from 310th Engineers, 337th Field Hospital, 337th Ambulance Company and three combat battalions of the 339th Infantry Regiment.

The main combat points between the Russian Red Army and the Allied forces would be among the main towns and villages along the Dvina, Vaga and Emtsa rivers and the railway line south of Archangel. These towns included Tulgas, Troitsa and Gorodok on the Dvina; Bereznik, Shenkursk and Ust-Padenga on the Vaga; Kodish and Avda on the Emtsa, Bolshie Ozerki, Emtsa and Plesetskaya on the railway front and a little further West the small but strategic town of Onega on the White Sea. These locations would become the frontlines for the battles to come, and they were among the destinations for the large number of troops arriving in Archangel during the Summer of 1918.

Chapter 2

Sgt John Agnew, 339th Infantry Regiment (Belfast)

The first Irishman to lose his life in the North Russian campaign was Sgt John Agnew of the 399th Infantry Brigade of the US Armed Forces. John Agnew was born in Belfast in December 1889 and was the first child of fitter David and Scottish-born Margaret Agnew. They would have another four children: two more sons, Robert and David, and two daughters, Martha and Jane. When John left school, he followed his father into the Fitter/Mechanic trade. When he reached the age of 21, John decided he wanted to spread his wings, and the following year, having saved the fare, he embarked from the port of Londonderry on board the SS *Columbia,* bound for New York. John then travelled to Boston and lived there for a while before moving to Detroit, where he thought the work opportunities were better. He managed to get a job as a shipping clerk in the prestigious department store of Crowley and Milner in downtown Detroit. John settled in Detroit and, in 1915, decided to apply for US citizenship by taking the first step, the 'Declaration of Intention'. This renounces any allegiance to any foreign 'prince, potentiate, state or sovereignty' before taking out US citizenship.

America entered WW1 in April 1917 following a spate of US merchant ships being sunk by Germany around the British Isles in the previous two years. Woodrow Wilson decided enough was enough and asked Congress for a 'war to end all wars'. On April 6th 1917, Congress voted to declare war on Germany, and the country began to mobilise its troops for service on the Western Front. Early the following year, an infantry regiment was raised in Detroit; John Agnew registered and was drafted into the 339th Infantry Regiment of the United States Army, popularly known as 'Detroit's Own'. Agnew trained for several months at Camp Custer in Michigan, was quickly promoted to Sergeant in "K" Company, and the regiment was then deemed ready for battle.

They left their training camp on July 14th and headed for Camp Mills in Long Island, from where they would leave for the Western Front. But by the time they boarded the transport ship, the USS *Harrisburg*, on July 22nd, their plans had changed, and they would now be heading for final training in the UK before proceeding to North Russia. Agnew also received news from Belfast that his mother Maggie had suffered a stroke, and her prospects, with regards to a recovery, were poor.

The USS Harrisburg that brought Sgt Agnew to the UK (NHHC).

The plan to reroute the Detroit 'doughboys' came about following President Wilson's agreement with his European allies that the US would send troops to Russia. Churchill had pleaded with the US to help with the intervention to restore the Eastern front, secure the armaments in Murmansk and Archangel, and maybe even reverse the communist revolution. Agnew's regiment planned to complete some final training in the UK and head for North Russia. The 339th Regiment was selected as it was believed that coming from Michigan, the soldiers making up this regiment would be better able to acclimatise themselves to the cold and harsh conditions of North Russia.

Following training in the UK, the 339th Regiment and ancillary units from the 85th Division set sail from Newcastle and arrived in Archangel on September 4th, 1918. The regiment came under the command of Major General Frederick Poole, Commander of the North Russia Expeditionary Force (NREF). The Americans who believed they were sent to North Russia for defensive purposes were now quickly disabused of this idea as, under British command, they were immediately sent to the river and railroad frontlines to continue with the offensive campaign against the Bolsheviks.

Archangel and surrounding area (Mike Grobbel)

Agnew's "K" company was transported by train down the Archangel/Vologda line towards Obozerskaya, but before reaching their destination, it was decided that two platoons of "K" company would enter the forest on the left and make their way through the forest heading southeast towards the river Emtsa. Their mission was to try to contact one of Major General Poole's combat teams – B Force – who had gone missing near Seletskoe and had not been heard of since late August. On the afternoon of 7th September 1918, Captain Michael Donoghue, with about 150 men (including Sgt. Agnew), entered the forest and headed in a southerly direction. After two days, they had traversed about 25 miles when they came upon freshly dug graves, and one of the men found a diary belonging to an American ensign with 'B Force', and the last entry in the diary was 30th August.[14] While it all sounded very ominous, the fact was that as O'Donoghue's men were reading the diary, they were unaware that the men they were looking for had already emerged from the forest and made contact with the Allied forces on the railway line from which O'Donoghue's men had just left. John Agnew was also unaware that his mother, who had suffered a stroke a couple of months previously, had passed away in her home in Delhi Street, Belfast.

The next two weeks saw Agnew tramping around in the forest led by O'Donoghue as they attempted to make inroads into the Bolshevik's position in the various towns along the Emtsa River. Both sides had blown up bridges spanning the river, and in late September, the Allies organised a force to take the town of Kodish on the east bank of the river, which the Bolsheviks controlled. The 'Kodish Force' numbered about 350 men and consisted of O'Donoghue's band of 'K' company troops, members of 'L' company, and several Machine Gun troops. The force, led by Lt. Charles Foster Chappel, was stationed on the west bank, and the plan called for wading across the river Emtsa, flanking the well-fortified town of Kodish and routing the Bolsheviks. The American troops were reluctant to carry out the plan as they believed they would be sitting ducks for the Bolshevik snipers as they made their way across the river on foot. Eventually, on the 27th of September, some rafts were located, and the Americans crossed the river in these rafts and dug in on the left and right flanks of Kodish. John Agnew was assigned to Lt. Chappel's group, who made the crossing on the left flank and came under very heavy fire while trying to attack one of the Bolshevik's machine-gun positions. Lt. Chappel was killed almost immediately, and before they could return to the safety of the river bank, another six soldiers, including John Agnew, had lost their lives. Lt. Charles Brady Ryan kept a diary of the event:

> *Started out about 5 AM and was with the main body at the bridge three versts outside of Kodish, ran into something, this proved to be a regular battle, there must be 1000 of them. I was on the right flank. The left caught it the heaviest. Lt. Chappel was killed and I guess also Sgt. Agnew, Sgt. Pease, Sgt. Nykus, Cpl. Dickey were all wounded... spent the night in the woods, walking around in water up to my knees.[15]*

Along with Sgt John Agnew and Lt. Chappel, the other US soldiers who died in the battle were Private Charles Vojta from Company 'K'; Cpl. Edward Mertens and Cpl. Edward Kreizinger of Company 'L' and Cpl. Harley Hester from the Machine Gun Company. As well as the six who lost their lives, another 24 troops were wounded in the battle, and later that day, Sgt. Emanuel Meister from the Machine Gun Company succumbed to his wounds. Sgt. Agnew and most of the other casualties were buried in the local cemetery in Seletskoe as the battle for Kodish continued relentlessly. After being reinforced by a detachment of the Royal Scots and one section of the Canadian field artillery, the Allies eventually took the town of Kodish on October 18th 1918.[16]

Aftermath

The news of John Agnew's death reached his family in Belfast, and a notice was placed in the Belfast Newsletter under the 'Roll of Honour' banner. As stated, John's mother, Maggie Agnew, died on 8th September, less than three weeks before her son was killed in Russia.

In 1934, the US sent a team to North Russia from Detroit to repatriate as many of the remains of the US war dead as possible, and Sgt John Agnew was one of the 14 sets of remains that were located and returned to the US that year. While many of those repatriated were buried at White Chapel Cemetery in Troy, Michigan, adjacent to the Polar Bear Monument,[17] Sgt Agnew's family in Belfast decided they would prefer he be reburied nearer home. It was agreed that he would be reinterred in the *Argonne American Cemetery* in Romagne, France.

Final resting place of Sgt John Agnew

John's father died in 1942, his youngest brother, David, in 1947 and his last surviving brother, Robert James, in 1958.

Chapter 3

Stoker 1st Class John Linton Beattie, Royal Navy
(Doneraile Co Cork)

John Linton Beattie was born in Doneraile, Co Cork, on 2nd February 1896 to George and Isabella Beattie. His parents, with two children (Christina and Robert), had emigrated to Doneraile from Ayr in Scotland in 1890. George was an experienced Sawyer, and work had become available in the newly established Sawmills in Doneraile. George and Isabella had another seven children (William, Archie, John, Jane, Annie, Tomas and Isabella) while they lived in Doneraile, and then they returned to Scotland in 1906, where they would have another two children (Catherine and Mary Jane), bringing the total number of children to eleven. While in Doneraile, George did well, working his way up to becoming the Mill Manager before changing occupations and becoming a 'hotel proprietor', having purchased the Imperial Hotel, Doneraile, from Mrs Ellen McCarthy in 1902. Then, in 1905, their daughter, six-year-old Jane, died suddenly, having taken ill with Laryngeal Diphtheria, which developed into pneumonia within 4 days, and she passed away in August 1905. Her heartbroken parents decided they had enough of Ireland and put the hotel up for sale the following month.

Within 6 months of the tragic loss of their daughter, the family were back in Newton-on-Ayr in Scotland. At 20 years of age, John Linton Beattie received a letter telling him he was to be conscripted into the military under the 1916 Military Service Act, which came into effect in January and made conscription compulsory for the first time since the beginning of the war. In his response, John indicated that he would prefer to serve with the Navy, which he was entitled to do under Section

20 of the Reserve Forces Act 1882; he was delighted when he was called up by the Admiralty in June 1916 and served aboard HMS *Victory* from June to November 1916 when he transferred to HMS *Dido* until July 1917. His final ship was HMS *Attentive* from January to his death in October 1918. During his time on HMS *Dido*, which was a depot ship to the 10th Destroyer Flotilla, he appeared to have disobeyed an order in some manner as he spent a month in 'Detention', which resulted in his annual character assessment being downgraded from 'VG' to 'Fair' on 31st December 1917.

After six months in the Royal Naval Barracks at Portsmouth, Beattie was assigned to HMS *Attentive* in January 1918, and this would prove to be his final assignment.

HMS *Attentive* **(IWM)**

HMS *Attentive* was one of a pair of 'Adventure' class scout cruisers built for the Royal Navy in the early part of the 20th century. *Attentive* spent most of her time during WW1 on coastal defence duties in the English Channel, but when Beattie joined her in 1918, he found himself involved in the Zeebrugge Raid whereby the RN attempted to block the Belgian port, which was in the control of the Germans, by sinking ships at the canal entrance (for more on this raid see the next chapter on Private Michael Keaveny). Following this mission, *Attentive* escorted convoys to Gibraltar before her final mission to Murmansk, supporting the Allied forces involved in the Russian Civil War.

As outlined previously, the Allies plan to invade Archangel came to fruition when a flotilla, under the command of Major General Poole and led by *HMS Attentive,* sailed into Archangel and, under covering fire from *Attentive,* a landing force took control of Archangel and martial law was declared by Poole. The success of this operation, taking control of a vast area by a small Allied contingent, meant that the Allied troops were spread very thinly on the ground. To counter this, in August 1918, Major General Poole requested that Naval Commander Admiral Kemp order the formation of a 'Russian Allied Naval Brigade' (RANB) consisting of local supportive Russians led and trained by Allied Naval personnel from HMS *Attentive*, USS *Olympia* and the French cruiser *Amiral Aube* and several Royal Marines. Stoker 1st Class John Linton Beattie was among the seven ratings selected from *Attentive* to be part of the Brigade leaders training the local Russians to defend North Russia against the Bolsheviks. The first recruits were formed into 'A' company and, following four weeks of training in Archangel, were dispatched 200km southwest to the town of Onega, situated at the mouth of the Onega River as it flows into the White Sea. In September 1918, Lt Colonel Patrick Edwards was ordered to take command of the Allied troops in the Onega area, and among the men who accompanied him was Stoker Beattie.

It's unclear what happened to John Beattie as the official report first lists him as 'reported missing 1-10-1918 during operations at Archangel' – a further entry in the report states that Stoker Beattie was 'taken prisoner of war by Russians "not missing"'. He was kept on the books of *Attentive* with full pay until the final notification from the Naval Personnel (NP) Division of the Admiralty on 7th December 1918 when he was on '1st October 1918 officially presumed to have lost his life during operations at Onega White Sea'. The likelihood is that the Bolsheviks took John Beattie prisoner, and he either died or was killed while in captivity.

Stoker Beattie did not have an official grave, so he is commemorated on the Archangel Memorial with 223 other names.

Aftermath

Acting Leading Stoker John Linton Beattie was entitled to the Victory and War medal, which his family duly claimed in the early 1920s. John's father, George Beattie, passed away on 7th October 1926, and his mother, Isabella, passed away in 1951. Descendants of the Beatty family still live in Ayr, Scotland.

Chapter 4

Pte Michael Keaveny, Royal Marine Light Infantry (Leitrim)

Michael Keaveny was born in Seltannaskeagh, in the Union of Manorhamilton, Co Leitrim, in June 1888. He came from a farming/industrial background, as his father worked as a 'road contractor' and then as a 'farmer' around the Lough Allen area. Michael was the fifth child of Michael (Sn) and Catherine (nee Lyons), who would have 11 children. Life was difficult for the Keaveny clan as they struggled to make a living from the scarce work available in Leitrim. Towards the end of the 19th century, it was popular for small farmers or cottiers to become seasonal harvest workers in Britain to make enough money to pay their rent.[18] After sowing his potato crop, Michael Keaveny (Sn) would emigrate to Scotland in late June to work as a harvester before returning to Leitrim in September to save the potato harvest and pay his rent from the money made in Scotland. Like many of the seasonal emigrants in or around 1910, the Keaveny family decided to emigrate fully to Scotland as it seemed a better location to make ends meet. They settled in Glencraig in Fife, and Michael (Sn) eventually became a grocery shop proprietor.

In 1911, young Michael was accepted as a trainee "Pupil Teacher" to be assigned to one of the Glasgow Catholic Schools experiencing an extreme shortage of teachers at the time. Because of this shortage, the Catholic hierarchy had allowed what they described as "Pupil Teachers" to make up the shortfall. These young instructors helped to relieve the pressure in the Catholic Schools around Glasgow, but because they lacked 'proper training and sufficient education themselves, they were often exploited'.[19]

It was a live-in system, and young Keaveny and another nine 'teachers' were based at 84 Henrietta Street in Glasgow, the former site of St Mary's Industrial School, which had relocated to Bishopbriggs in 1901. When war broke out in 1914, Keaveny was still teaching in a Catholic school in Glasgow and studying for his final examinations. In May 1915, he received news that his father had died in Glencraig and travelled back there for the funeral and burial in Ballingry New Cemetery.

On his return to Glasgow, he found it hard to settle back into the strict and restrictive life as a Catholic school teacher. In February 1917, he was called up for military service and enlisted in the Royal Marine Light Infantry (RMLI). Following basic training at the recruit depot in Deal, Keaveny then spent three months of further training at Plymouth, from whence he was assigned to the 4th Royal Marines Battalion for a special amphibious operation planned by the Admiralty. The main objective of this daring plan was to block the ports of Zeebrugge and Ostend by scuttling concrete-filled ships in the mouths of both harbours. Keaveny was attached to 'C' company, a seaborne assault unit tasked with the secondary objective of attacking and damaging the 'Mole' at Zeebrugge.

The 'Mole' was a mile-long granite seawall jutting out into the North Sea with artillery protecting the port of Zeebrugge, which was used as a safe harbour for the U-boats that were wreaking havoc on Allied shipping during the war. On 22nd April, HMS *Vindictive*, with Keaveny and 'C' company aboard, left the UK and headed for the Belgian coast and Zeebrugge. Because the Royal Navy did not have an established seaborne raiding force, the 'Zeebrugge Raiders' were all volunteers for the operation at hand. The plan called for an initial bombardment of the port followed by a smokescreen to allow *'Vindictive'* to land the assault force on the Mole without being seen. Just as this was about to happen, the wind changed, blowing the smoke away from *'Vindictive'*, and the disembarking troops, which included Keaveny, became exposed to the

German machine guns. One survivor, Sergeant Harry White, described the scene:

Up the ramp we dashed, carrying our ladders and ropes, passing our dead and wounded lying everywhere, and the big gaps made in the ship's decks by shellfire. Finally, we crossed the two remaining gangways, which were only just hanging together, and jumped onto the concrete wall, only to find it swept by machine-gun fire. Our casualties were so great before the landing that of a platoon of 45 men only 12 landed.[20]

Unfortunately, Keaveny was one of these casualties and suffered a 'shrapnel wound' to the head, for which he was treated and recovered within a couple of months. Militarily, the Zeebrugge raid was unsuccessful, as the blockade lasted less than a week before the port was cleared, but morally and for propaganda purposes, it was a huge success. Eight Victoria Crosses were won at Zeebrugge, and interestingly, Keaveny's 4th Royal Marine's Battalion was awarded the Victoria Cross as a group but, as this was against the rules, the Battalion voted that Captain Edward Bamford and Sgt Norman Finch would each be given the VC and this was duly agreed. The citation to Bamford tells the story:

For conspicuous gallantry at Zeebrugge. April 1918. This officer landed on the Mole from "Vindictive" with Nos. 5, 7 & 8 platoons of the Marine Storming Force in the face of great difficulties. When on the Mole under heavy fire, he displayed the greatest initiative in the command of his company, and by his total disregard of danger, showed a magnificent example to his men. He first established a strong point on the right of the disembarkation, and when that was safe, led an assault on a battery to the left with the utmost coolness and valour. Captain Bamford was selected by the officers of the R.M.A & R.M.L.I detachments to receive the Victoria Cross under Rule 13 of the Royal Warrant, dated 26 January 1856.[21]

The citation for Finch likewise provides the context:

For most conspicuous gallantry. Sergeant Finch was second in command of the pompoms and Lewis guns in the foretop of Vindictive, under Lieutenant Charles N. B. Rigby, R.M.A. At one period the Vindictive was being hit every few seconds, chiefly in the upper works, from which splinters caused many casualties. It was difficult to locate the guns which were doing the most damage, but Lieutenant Rigby, Sergeant Finch and the Marines in the foretop, kept up a continuous fire with pompoms and Lewis guns, changing rapidly from one target to another, and thus keeping the enemy's fire down to some considerable extent. Unfortunately, two heavy shells made direct hits on the foretop, which was completely exposed to enemy concentration of fire. All in the top were killed or disabled except Sergeant Finch, who was, however, severely wounded; nevertheless, he showed consummate bravery, remaining in his battered and exposed position. He once more got a Lewis gun into action, and kept up a continuous fire, harassing the enemy on the mole, until the foretop received another direct hit, the remainder of the armament being then completely put out of action. Before the top was destroyed Sergeant Finch had done invaluable work, and by his bravery undoubtedly saved many lives. This very gallant sergeant of the Royal Marine Artillery was selected by the 4th Battalion of Royal Marines, who were mostly Royal Marine Light Infantry, to receive the Victoria Cross under Rule 13 of the Royal Warrant dated 29th January, 1856.[22]

Following his recovery from the shrapnel head wound in May 1918, Keaveny was assigned to HMS *Glory* for patrol duties in North Russia. '*Glory*' had been on duty in North Russia since August 1916 as the flagship for the British North Russian Squadron, under Rear-Admiral Thomas Kemp, to protect the armaments being sent to aid the Russians in their war on the Eastern Front. Following the Russian Revolution, the need to protect the armaments became more acute as the Bolsheviks sought a peace agreement with the Central Powers to take them out of the war. Following the Treaty of Brest-Litovsk in March 1918, the Armaments needed to be protected now from the Bolsheviks as well, and for this reason, the British began to reinforce their forces in Murmansk.

Because of the dire situation on the Western Front, the British Army was unable to send troops to Murmansk. In May 1918, the Admiralty decided to send a small force of Royal Marines to hold Murmansk and… secure the railway and the White Sea ports.[23] Keaveny was a member of this unit, and after being equipped with both summer and winter clothing, they set sail from Newcastle on board SS *Porto* on May 20, 1918, arriving in Murmansk nine days later. The unit was known as *Glory III* as it was borne on the books of HMS *Glory*. Following their arrival, they occupied several buildings in Murmansk that became known as the Royal Marines' Barracks.

Keaveny, together with another 150 NCOs, was sent 350 miles south to Kem under the command of Captain Drake-Brockman to restore order as the area was experiencing a lot of unrest due to the activities of the Finnish White Guards that had crossed the border into Northern Russia. Because the Germans supported the Finnish Whites, the British, in turn, placed their support on the Finnish Reds, particularly the ethnic Karelian population, who straddled the border between Finland and Russia. Captain Drake-Brockman had been promoted to the local rank of Major to recruit and lead the Karelians against the Finnish Whites, which he did and restored order to the area. Around this time (July 1918), US President Woodrow Wilson finally yielded to the British pleadings to intervene in Russia. He agreed to send American troops to support the British and French, who were already ensconced there. While the Americans brought weapons and troops to the theatre of war, they also brought something else – Spanish Flu.

It is believed that the Spanish flu originated in Haskell County, Kansas, in late January 1918. It quickly spread 300 miles west to Funston Army Camp in Fort Riley and, from there, to other army camps around the

US.[24] As the American troops were being shipped to the Western Front, it wasn't long until outbreaks of Spanish flu reached Europe; it is estimated that between 50 and 100 million people died worldwide because of the pandemic.[25] According to the log of the HMS *Glory*, there seem to be two spikes in sick-bay numbers that, more than likely, can be attributed to the arrival of the Spanish Flu in Russia. The first occurred in May 1918 when the numbers on the sick list climbed from an average of 7 or 8 per day to more than 100 before returning to normal levels again one week later. The second spike occurred in late September 1918, lasted for several weeks, and resulted in many fatalities in October and November of the same year. Keaveny fell ill and died on 4th October 1918, and while the death is recorded as from 'illness' and from 'disease', it more than likely was from the Spanish flu that was raging at the time. Private Michael Keaveny was given a full military funeral and buried in Kem Cemetery, North Russia.

Pte Michael Keaveny's freshly dug grave October 1918 (IWM).

This grave is now lost to time. However, in 1930, the Commonwealth War Graves Commission (CWGC) created the Murmansk New British Cemetery and 40 burials were moved from the old cemetery used by No. 86 General Hospital during the intervention years. The new cemetery now contains 83 burials and commemorations of the Great War. Included in the commemorations is Special Memorial B.15 to Private Keaveny.

Aftermath

In 1923, Michael's mother, Catherine, emigrated to America with her 19-year-old son Aiden. She lived in the Bronx with her son Austin, but when Aiden got married in 1927, Catherine lived with him until she died in 1947, aged 79; she was buried in Old St Raymond's cemetery in the Bronx. Many of the other siblings of Michael Keaveny emigrated to the US, including Mary Jane (Mollie) and her husband John McKenna, Patrick, James, Catherine, John and, as previously stated, Austin and Aiden. Joseph and Anne remained in Scotland.

It was about this time (early October 1918), prior to the closing of the port, that HMS *Attentive* entered Archangel with a most interesting character on board. Major General Edmond Ironside was nicknamed 'Tiny' because he was 6 foot 4 inches tall and weighed 19 stone. He was sent to North Russia as Chief of Staff to General Poole, who, a week later, on 14th October 1918, was recalled to London for 'consultations' with the War Office.[26] Ironside has been described as:

> *...six feet four inches tall without shoes, weighs 270 pounds, and is only thirty-seven years old. He is descended from the last Saxon king of England, was dismissed from St Andrew's School when he was 10½ years old because he whipped the teacher. He was the first British officer to land in France; in fact, he landed on August 2, before England entered the war on August 6 [sic]. He was in command of a division on the French front when he was ordered to Russia. He relinquished his command and cleared in an aeroplane*

for England. After a flight of three and one-half hours he landed somewhere in England, spent three days acquainting himself with Russian conditions and left for Archangel; he does everything that way.[27]

The first thing Ironside did on assuming command was to check out the troops on the various active fronts before the rivers and port began to freeze over and movement became restricted.

Chapter 5

Lt William Frederick Bassett Black Watch, att. 2/10th Royal Scots (Waterford)

The next Irishman to be killed during the North Russian Intervention was a British Army Lieutenant from Waterford. William Bassett was born in the City of Waterford on March 22, 1883. His father, George, worked as an accountant in the port area of Waterford, and his mother, Sara, worked as a schoolteacher until her marriage to George in 1877. The Bassetts had eight children, and William came fourth, meaning he had three older brothers, three younger brothers and one younger sister.

The family fortunes took a turn for the better when the father decided to go into the wine business and established Messrs. Bassett and Meredith, Wine Merchants on Parade Quay in Waterford, which became one of the leading wine merchants in the southeast of the country. William was a diligent student and a hard worker; in 1903, he was appointed a second-division clerk in the civil service. A few years later (1905), he was promoted to the registry of Deeds (Ireland) offices in Dublin, where he stayed until he enlisted in the Black Watch (Royal Highlanders) at the outbreak of the Great War and, following training in Scotland, was appointed 2nd Lieutenant in April 1916. He then embarked for Salonika in November 1916 and took part in the Balkans' campaign. Bassett also served on the Western Front and, in June 1918, found himself back in Ireland attached to the 2/10th Royal Scots Battalion. The 2/10th had spent the best part of the war on 'coastal duties' in Britain because many of the enlisted men had been deemed physically unfit for front-line duty – this was either due to the poor physical condition of the soldiers or as a result of wounds received in battle. On the other hand, a number of the officers of the Royal Scots were battle-hardened from service on the Western Front and had been sent to the 2/10th for a 'rest' from frontline duties. William Bassett was one of those officers who had seen some fierce action in the Balkans and on the Western Front, and his attachment to the Royal Scots was an attempt to offer him a respite from the front line to recharge his batteries.

While back in Ireland, William was able to catch up on family news, particularly on his four brothers, who had emigrated to Canada prior to the outbreak of the war. In 1905, his elder brother Herbert John emigrated to Canada on the SS *Numidian*, and in 1910, his brothers Benjamin and Thomas joined him in Montreal. They sailed out of Liverpool on board the SS *Canada*, and Benjamin described his occupation as a chemist while Thomas described himself as a labourer.

Shortly after settling in Montreal, they persuaded another brother, Richard Stanley, to join them in Canada. At the outbreak of the war, three brothers enlisted with the Canadian forces while Herbert, who was married and living in the city of Galt, Ontario, decided to stay out of the war. Benjamin, Thomas, and Richard joined the 52nd (New Ontario) Battalion, which was raised in the Port Arthur region of Ontario. They embarked from Montreal on board the SS *Missanabie* bound for England before being sent to the Western Front. Both Benjamin and Richard were awarded 'Good Conduct' badges, and Richard was awarded the Military Medal for bravery in 1917. Because of his medical training, Benjamin was transferred to the 1st Canadian Field Ambulance, serving there until the war's end.

Benjamin Bassett (Kenora War Project)

Following William's posting to Ireland and catching up with the family news, the situation in North Russia began to deteriorate due to the lack of reinforcements, and it was decided that the Royal Scots should be strengthened and prepared for action in Russia. Replacements were found for the less able soldiers, and 2nd Lieutenant Bassett saw the Battalion considerably strengthened before leaving Ireland for Aldershot and then embarking from Newcastle for Archangel on board the SS *City of Cairo*. They disembarked on 25th August 1918 and, following a parade through the main thoroughfare of Archangel, were immediately dispatched 200 miles up the River Dvina on barges to confront the Red Army, who were reinforcing the Bolsheviks that had recently been ejected from the city. It took the barges five days to reach their goal, the village of Bereznik, from where operations against the Bolsheviks would be conducted. The Royal Scots were part of a more considerable force whose objective was to push the Bolsheviks out of the villages along the banks of the Dvina running southeast of Bereznik. It was hoped that the White Russians might thus become emboldened by these successes and turn the tide against the Red Army and the Communist revolution of 1917.

Not long after their arrival in Bereznik, the Royal Scots came under attack by the Bolsheviks and, after repelling the attack, continued to pursue the 'Reds' along the Dvina, capturing several prisoners and a couple of guns – 76.2mm M02 Putilovs – one (the Archangel Gun) of which was brought back to Scotland and is now located at Dreghorn Barracks in Edinburgh.

The 'Archangel Gun' in 1919 at Glencorse Barracks.(photo taken by Henry Myers in 1919 available at http://www.staffshomeguard.co.uk/)

The 'Archangel Gun' in 2012 at Dreghorn Barracks (photograph reproduced with the kind permission of the Royal Scots Museum)

Following this successful initial battle with the enemy, the following months saw slower progress as the Royal Scots and a company of American troops attempted to clear a large triangle below the confluence of the Dvina and Vaga rivers. Some better-fortified villages could not be attacked in a frontal assault, so a flanking approach was taken. This necessitated some gruelling marches through thick swampy forests, and the troops were often exhausted when they reached their objective.

In early October 1918, the 'Dvina Force' had managed to clear the triangle from Bereznik to Borok on the Dvina and to Shenkursk on the river Vaga, but they were coming under increasing retaliatory attacks from a large force of Bolsheviks who were regrouping and probing the Allied forces. Lieutenant William Bassett showed exemplary courage in these battles and was awarded the Military Cross (MC) for his bravery and leadership under fire. The citation records the story:

> *While in command of the Right Bank outpost line at Higher Borok, consisting of two platoons and an additional Lewis gun section,*

he was twice attacked by greatly superior numbers of the enemy. Although his position was being heavily shelled and the village set on fire, with great fearlessness he walked round his posts encouraging his men and directing their fire, so that the enemy attacks were smashed and his pursuing patrols were able to capture a machine gun. On the following morning, when the enemy attempted a further attack, he was a splendid example of coolness and courage.[28]

Later in the month, on the 27th of October 1918, another flanking operation was undertaken, this time at dawn against the village of Topsa. Lieutenant William Bassett was again involved in the march through the dense forest, but the conditions worsened as a blinding snowstorm was underway. The Bolsheviks who had retaken Topsa had learned a valuable lesson and were now well prepared for outflanking manoeuvres. Without the element of surprise, the Royal Scots suffered heavy casualties, including 26 other ranks and one officer – Lt. William Bassett - killed. An eyewitness, John Buchan, tells the story:

The 27th October saw a mixed force of one hundred and twenty Royal Scots, forty Poles, and twenty Russian scouts set out to drive the enemy from a commanding position held by him at Topsa, five versts away from our right-bank position. Setting out at 11 p.m., the force marched through a snowstorm with slush under foot, and took up its attacking position at 6 am. Presumably, the enemy had been previously warned, or possibly the barking of village dogs had alarmed him, for no sooner had one of his sentries given the alarm than our men were assailed by machine-gun fire which held them up. This was followed up by attacks on both our flanks, and soon our force was pushed back, the fight being maintained by parties of men, most of the officers having become early casualties. The failure of this attack resulted in losses to us of eighty all ranks in killed, missing, wounded, and prisoners. The remainder made their way back with difficulty through marsh and forest.[29]

Lt William Bassett was buried, along with the other casualties of the battle, near where they were killed. It would take another week before the devastating news was relayed back to his parents in Waterford, and they were heartbroken that he would be buried in the field so far from home.

Aftermath

As for the remainder of the Bassett brothers who served in the colours, his brother Benjamin finished out the war in Europe but decided not to return to Canada and instead returned to Ireland and settled in Rathmines where in 1922, he married Nora Taylor, and they had three children William, Pamela, and Patricia. They owned and operated the Rathmines Pharmacy, which they ran until Benjamin's retirement – he died in 1974 and is buried in St. Andrew Cemetery in Malahide.

Richard returned to Canada, but in 1922, he emigrated to the United States, working for the Delaware Company as a salesman. He married his Canadian sweetheart Alberta Brownell in 1927, and they had one child, Frances Sheila, who was born in 1929 but tragically died, aged 6, in 1935. Richard died in Doylestown, Pennsylvania, in 1977, and his wife Alberta died in 1980. The final brother who served in the army was Thomas, who returned to Canada after the war, married Christina Finlay, had one child, George Finlay Bassett and died in 1959.

Because Lt William Frederick Bassett was buried near the village of Topsa and the grave is now lost to time, he is commemorated on the Archangel memorial with another 223 members of the intervention force whose graves are no longer accessible.

Archangel Memorial

In October 1924, Lt William Bassett was remembered in the Irish Times newspaper with the following inscription:

> **ROLL OF HONOUR.**
> (1914-1918.)
> In Memoriam.
> BASSETT—In proud and loving memory of Lieutenant W. F. Bassett, M.C., 10th Black Watch (attached 2nd Battalion Royal Scots), killed in action, North Russia, 27th October, 1918. "I thank my God on every remembrance of you."

Winter and the sub-Arctic temperature were now in full swing, and many Allied troops were questioning why they remained in North Russia despite the end of the Great War. In particular, the American troops (the Polar Bears) felt aggrieved that they found themselves in combat duties despite the promise that they were just there to guard the military stores in Archangel. The next Irish-born casualty in North Russia was one of those troops serving with a US Infantry Regiment.

Chapter 6

Sgt. Michael Kenney, 339ᵗʰ Infantry Regiment (Sligo)

Sgt Michael Kenney (public domain)

Born on the 30ᵗʰ of November 1890, Michael Cunney [30] was the second child to John and his wife Bridget. Bridget and John would go on to have six children in total: Pat (1889), Michael (1890), Anne (1892), Catherine (1894), John (1896) and Mary Ellen (1900). The family had a small holding in the townland of Carraun, Co Sligo, close to the Mayo border. It was a hard life, and as soon as the eldest son, Pat, reached 18, he emigrated to America, where he found work in Chicago as a labourer. The sisters Ann and Catherine (Kate) were next to go in 1913. They settled in New York and worked as domestics in some of the wealthy houses on the upper west side of Manhattan. When Michael left school, he went to work with his father on the farm, but in his mid-twenties, he decided to follow in his sisters and brother's footsteps and emigrated to America.

Michael didn't join his sisters in New York or his brother in Chicago but instead opted for Detroit, Michigan, where his cousin, John Freeman, was making a comfortable living as a moulder in the burgeoning car industry. When Michael arrived in Detroit, he found work in the Studebaker Corporation. He was a good worker, and before long, he was promoted to 'Stock Foreman' in this thriving car-making factory.

When the US declared war on Germany in April 1917, the recruitment drive did not raise the numbers needed for quick training and deployment overseas. For this reason, on May 18th 1917, Congress passed the Selective Service Act, which initially required all males aged between 20 and 30 to register for military service (the draft was soon expanded to include all able-bodied males aged 18-35). This would result in 2.8 million men being inducted into the US military in the next two years.[31]

Michael Kenney duly registered on 5th June 1917 but wasn't drafted until the end of the year. He joined the 339th Infantry Regiment, popularly known as 'Detroit's Own'. Following 6 months of training at Camp Custer, Michigan, he was promoted to Sergeant in 'K' company of the 339th Infantry Regiment. In July 1918, the Regiment headed for Camp Mills on Long Island, New York, to catch a boat to Europe and the Western Front. Before embarking on a trip to Europe, Michael, or Mick, as he was known to his family, got a weekend pass and travelled to Manhattan to meet up with his sister Ann. A photo was taken as a memento of the occasion.

Sgt Michael Kenney and his sister Ann (JE Walsh)

The 339th Infantry was informed of a change of plan; instead of the Western Front, they would now be posted to North Russia as part of the Allied Interventionist force assembling there. First, they would travel to Camp Cowshott in Surrey, where they would be assembled and equipped for the harsh conditions in North Russia. They boarded the USS Harrisburg on July 22 for transportation to England. It is more than probable that Sgt Kenney had become a good friend of Sgt Agnew (see Chapter 2) as they were both in 'K' company, both Irish, and both had been promoted to Sergeant following training at Camp Custer. On the passenger list of the USS Harrisburg, they are listed together.

5	AGNEW, JOHN	2021637	SGT		MRS. DAVID AGNEW	MOTH	91 DELHI ST., BELFAST, IRELAND.
6	KENNEY, MICHAEL J.	2021671	SGT		MR. JOHN FREEMAN	COUS	1029 GRAND RIVER AVE., DETROIT, MICH.

Passenger list of the USS Harrisburg that sailed for England in July 1918

Following two weeks in Surrey, the 339th Infantry Regiment became part of the American Expeditionary Force (AEF). It sailed for North Russia from the port city of Newcastle upon Tyne on the 27th of August and landed in Archangel on the 4th of September 1918.

Immediately, 'K' company was sent south by train to protect the railway line from the Bolsheviks. Kenney was awarded the first of two medals for gallantry and bravery in the ensuing battles. The citation provides the story:

> *On the 16ᵗʰ September 1918 [Kenney] withheld a vigorous flank attack upon the village of Seletskoe. By his coolness of thought, energy and steadfastness in the direction of his detachment of 15 men, outnumbered tenfold, he prevented a movement and an attempt to occupy commanding ground by the enemy, the success of which would have been disastrous to the Allied troops then defending the village.*[32]

Following the defence of Seletskoe, Sgt Kenney and 'K' company were then ordered to take the town of Kodish, which lay south of Seletskoe on the opposite side of the Emtsa River. The battle for Kodish over the winter months of 1918 seemed to epitomise the futility of the Russian intervention as the Allies took the town, then lost it to the Bolsheviks, and this operation was repeated time and time over these frozen months. It would take months for the Allies to realise that 'the town of Kodish was worthless for their purposes and was strategically untenable'.[33] Kenney was involved in the October direct attack in Kodish, and for his actions in this battle, he won his second award for bravery:

> *The energy and dash of his grenadiers, due to his keenness, bravery, and coolness under the most hazardous conditions, was largely responsible for the success of the Allied force in the attack and capture of the village of Kodish on Oct. 12ᵗʰ and 13ᵗʰ, 1918.*[34]

Following the armistice in Europe, the American troops were hoping to be sent home now that the war was over, but they were quickly disabused of this idea as the fighting and battles raged on for a further 7 months before the US soldiers were finally withdrawn in July 1919. However, for those 7 months, the American troops must have asked themselves, 'Why are we here?'. A letter written by Captain Robert Boyd of the 339ᵗʰ Infantry captures this sentiment precisely:

One question which is asked by the intelligent enlisted man, and I ask it of myself.......While a state of war existed with Germany our mission, ostensibly at least, was to create an Eastern front against Germany by developing a new Russian army. That state of war is now over, and I have always thought it one of our national policies that the settlement of internal dissensions in a foreign country, if not interfering with our national rights, was inherent with their power of self-government. If that is the case, what moral justification have the Allied forces, and particularly our own, in Russia since the cessation of hostilities? If it is not the case what is our national policy here?

There has been no open dissatisfaction, the men have gone through hardships and fighting cheerfully, but will soon begin to say among themselves, "why are we here." It is my business to answer that question and I cannot.[35]

By December 1918, the town of Kodish had again fallen to the Bolsheviks, and the Allies decided to try and retake it and also the town of Avda, which lay west of Kodish. Murmurings of discontent were heard from the American troops as they were told of the plans; Lt Ryan wrote in his diary about the attack on Kodish: ' We are to make another advance. The same old stuff. We made it once, got chased back, and now we will try again. This winter campaign is going to be hard on the men.'[36] According to Halliday, 'From a strictly military point of view, the operation on the Kodish front at the very end of 1918 was a puny affair. A few hundred Americans went out into the snow and the darkness and took an insignificant Russian village (Kodish), held it for a while and gave it up again to the enemy.[37] The 30th December 1918 was the date set for the 'big push', and Sgt Kenney's K company and L and E companies were to lead the infantry advance. At 6.00 am, the morning lit up from artillery and mortar fire, and following this shelling, the infantry started their advance on Kodish. It was expected that the town of Kodish would fall rapidly, and the troops would then take the sister- village of Avda. However, the Bolsheviks put up stiff resistance, and it wasn't until 6.00

pm that Kodish fell to the Allies. The push then began for Avda, but the Bolsheviks had prepared for the fall of Kodish by setting up some strategic ambush sites for the Allies:

> *'Kodish was in a hollow, with hills on three sides, and it consequently was more easily attacked than defended. The Bolsheviks had previously constructed machine-gun dugouts at strong points along the road south of the town, and from these, they subjected the advancing American platoons to a destructive fire'* [38]

It was nearing midnight on the 30th of December when K company were forced to halt briefly in the snow after battling their way down the road towards Avda. Sgt Kenney 'went the rounds encouraging the men, weary after eighteen hours of almost continuous fighting. He told them a quick skirmish in Avda, and they'd have houses to sleep in and warm fires. As he was making his rounds, a burst of Bolshevik machine-gun fire hit Kenney in the neck and chest. He was quickly brought to the safety of a makeshift hospital in the local church, where he died.

A soldier who stayed with Mick later told his family '...that for a while Mick stayed conscious and could talk, but said little. At about three in the morning on New Year's Eve, he whispered some words that sounded like "Happy New Year." Then he closed his eyes and died'.[39] Sgt Michael Kenney's remains were transported back to Archangel, where he was buried in the Allied Cemetery there.

In June 1919, the Americans began their withdrawal from North Russia, and by the end of the month, they were all gone.[40] In November, the remains of Sgt Michael Kenney and 112 other American soldiers and seamen were transported on the *SS Daraga* from Archangel to Hoboken in New Jersey. While most of the casualties were buried in the White Chapel Cemetery under the Polar Bear Memorial in Michigan, some families chose to have their loved ones interred closer to their homes. Michael Kenney's sister Ann decided to have his remains laid to rest in Calvery Cemetery, Queens, New York.

Aftermath

Two of Michael's siblings remained in Ireland, his youngest brother John inherited the farm, and in 1932, he married Margaret Seery; they had two children, Tom and Beatrice, and both emigrated to the US. Mary Ellen, the youngest of the Cunney family, married William Henry in 1931, and they also had two children, Jack and Kate; this family remained in Sligo. Michael's older brother Pat, who had emigrated to the US in 1907, settled in Chicago and worked for the Clinton Realty Association. He married Catherine (Kate) Nealon and had three children: Margaret, John and Donald. Pat died in October 1949 and is buried in Saint Mary's Catholic Cemetery and Mausoleum in Chicago.

Mike's youngest sister, Kate, emigrated to the US with her sister Anne and settled in New York; she married Michael J Henry and had two children, Joan and Margaret. Anne, Mike's final sister, who had the professional photograph taken in 1918, settled in New York, married Thomas Walsh in 1923 and had four children: Patricia, Thomas, John, and William. Their son, John Evangelist Walsh (1927-2015), would become a distinguished author of over a dozen books. He is best known for leading a team of 7 editors in the quest to create a condensed version of the Bible. Sgt Michael Kenney (1890 – 1918) is commemorated on the Sentinel Stones of the Great War Memorial Garden in Co. Sligo.

Meanwhile, back in Russia following the death of Sgt Kenney, the port of Archangel was now icebound and would remain so until April of the following year. However, being isolated and icebound didn't mean things quietened as hostilities continued along the frontlines into the new year. It was in the early part of 1919 that the next Irish-born casualty lost his life when his RAF plane went down behind enemy lines.

Chapter 7

Second Lt. Noel Daniel Nunan, Royal Air Force
(Blarney Co. Cork)

2ⁿᵈ Lt Noel Daniel Nunan (RAF Museum)

Noel Daniel Nunan was born in Blarney in December 1892 to Dr Francis and Hanna Nunan. Daniel was the second eldest boy, one of 11 children, six girls and five boys. His father, who was the registrar for the area, was also the dispensary medical officer. Civil registration of births began in Ireland in 1864, and registrars were appointed in various districts around Ireland to record births and deaths in their area. Francis Nunan was appointed Registrar for the Blarney district. Consequently, as well as having his name as the father on his son's birth certificate, Francis was also the person who registered Noel's birth as part of his official duties (see below).

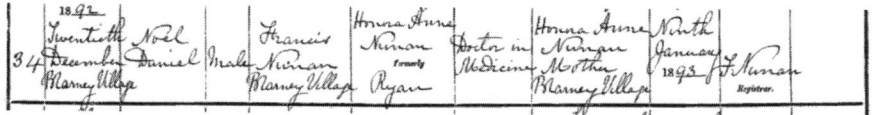

Francis Nunan entered as Father and Registrar on Noel's birth certificate

Following his primary schooling in Blarney and then the Christian Brothers College in Cork, Noel began training as a mechanic. Shortly after completing his training, he decided to emigrate to Canada and link up with his older brother Francis Joseph, who had emigrated there in 1910. Noel sailed from Liverpool on 14th February 1913 on board the SS *Tunisian*, heading for St John's, Newfoundland. Shortly after, a younger sibling, Alfred John, decided to join his brothers in Canada. On the ship's passenger list, Noel classified himself as a mechanic, while his brother stated he was a farmhand. After spending some time with Francis, Noel and Alfred moved eastwards and made their way to Calgary, where they found jobs in their respective fields.

The Canadian Federal Government aimed to settle the North Eastern territories at the time. It encouraged Europeans and Canadians to apply for plots of land (160 acres) under the Dominion Lands Act (1872). The Nunan brothers became interested in applying for a plot of land under the above Act, but when war broke out in Europe in August 1914, they instead thought about enlisting. In January 1915, Alfred enlisted and embarked for Europe (Plymouth, England) the following October.

In August 1915, Noel applied for and was granted a plot of land about 60 km northwest of Grande Prairie in Alberta. On being granted the land, the homesteader was expected to clear a portion of the land, undertake some cultivation, build a house and a barn and live there for at least six months each year for three years. On 'proving up' his or her plot of land, the homesteader could then apply for the title to the land.[41] Noel attempted to clear and improve the land he was granted, but the work proved too difficult for one person. After surrendering the plot of land, he returned to mechanical work in the nearby town of Grande Prairie. Meanwhile, his brother Alfred wrote to Noel about his exploits since arriving in England.

Shortly after he arrived in Plymouth, Alfred was granted leave to travel home to Blarney for Christmas 1915. While spending some time with his family, Alfred fell ill and was treated in St Anne's Hydro in Blarney, which at the time was being used by the military as a hospital for convalescing soldiers. He spent a month in St Anne's and was transferred to the Central Military Hospital in Victoria Barracks, Cork. He was discharged from hospital in February 1916 to rejoin his unit in Britain, and in August, he proceeded to France and the Western Front.

The letter from Alfred reawakened Noel's resolve to enlist in the Canadian army, but before he did, he reapplied for another plot of land as he learned that potential homesteaders may be granted the patent for the land without having to make improvements, provided they were on military duties for their country over the three years. In March 1916, Noel applied for a plot of land, and on the 23rd of March, he got the news that his application was successful, being granted a plot at NW 4-73-11-W6 near the town of Hythe in Alberta. Two days later, Noel presented himself at the Grande Prairie enlistment office and joined the 194th Battalion of the Canadian Expeditionary Forces. Following 8 months of training, Noel was assigned to the 49th Battalion (Edmonton Regiment), went overseas on the SS *Olympic*, and saw action on the Western Front as a signaller, which meant he was involved in military communications.

On April 14th, 1917, Noel was severely wounded in the left leg by sniper fire and spent a couple of weeks in hospital before being shipped to Britain and the City of London Royal Hospital in Clapton for further treatment. Following his recovery, he did not return to the front lines but remained in England and was transferred to various Reserve Battalions stationed around Bramshott. His final unit was the 21st Reserve Battalion, when he requested a transfer to the Royal Flying Corps as a cadet. His request was granted on 5th March 1918, and he attended a pilot training school at Frith Hill, Blackdown, Surrey, as a member of the Royal Flying Corps but still attached to the 21st Reserve Battalion. After completing preliminary tests in late June 1918, Nunan was discharged from the 21st Canadian Reserve Battalion (Alberta) and enlisted in the Royal Air Force (Royal Flying Corps became the Royal Air Force on April 1st 1918) on being appointed a Flight Cadet. Nunan and eighty other cadets were the first group to join the fledging Royal Air Force (RAF). He went for further training in Woking in August 1918. Then, he had to complete a series of final tests, which consisted of an exercise in the air, the pilot being the examiner, and three written exams, which he passed easily.

On completion, he was granted a temporary commission as 2nd Lieutenant (Observer Officer) in September 1918. He was then assigned to 'ELOPE' squadron to serve in Archangel North Russia as an RAF Observer. The squadron, comprising 1,300 Canadian, British, and French troops, embarked from Dundee with an escort at 3.00 pm on 21st September 1918, bound for Archangel. The ship was overloaded with troops, and the nine uncomfortable days it took to get there saw many succumb to sickness:

> *The sea was rough and many on board were seasick. Influenza and pneumonia developed among the crowded troops, one French soldier dying and being buried at sea. The destroyer escort left the convoy at the Shetland Islands, and from then on, the convoy zig-zagged alone through the cold, deserted waters of the Arctic Ocean.*[42]

Lt Nunan finally reached Archangel on October 1, and the RAF personnel were divided into three groups. The first group was sent to the Pinega front, east of Archangel, while Nunan was assigned to "A" Flight on the railway front. The last group, "B" Flight, was sent down the River Dvina to the front lines. After two weeks of acclimatisation in Archangel, Nunan proceeded to Obozerskaya on the Railway front, about 100 miles south of Archangel.

Later, Nunan's "A" Flight was assigned to RAF 'No. 4 Squadron' based in Obozerskaya and shared the base with the 'Slavo-British Aviation Corps' consisting of experienced Russian pilots but having no aircraft. These two branches of the British Air Corps cooperated to provide air cover for the area around their base. The cover usually involved bombing raids, reconnaissance, and assisting operations on the ground. When the armistice was signed on November 11, the troops in North Russia were quickly disabused of any ideas of the war being over for them. Lt Frank Shrive, like Nunan, an RAF observer, explained in his diary how they were informed of the armistice:

> *Captain Albu, our Flight Commander, had just called us together. He said I have some good news for you and also some which is not so good. First, an Armistice has been signed and the war is over. This took place at eleven a.m. yesterday. Now, he said, as far as he knew this would not affect the North Russian expedition and until further word was received, we were to carry on according to orders. This second announcement did not surprise us much as we had discussed this probability quite often previously and were not too surprised.*[43]

Located in Obozerskaya, Lt Noel Nunan mainly flew the two-seater 'Sopwith,' often called a 'Sop One-and-a-Half-Strutter.' It got this name from the long and short cabane struts that support the top wing.

Sopwith 1½ Strutter (public domain)

Continuous action around the railway front was relieved by the occasional trip to Archangel for badly needed rest and relaxation. But as one RAF observer claimed: 'Leave in Archangel is not like leave in London'. With only one 'picture show', mainly out-of-date films, the only other social event was the 'Officer's Club', which remained open until midnight.

> *This is a popular spot as we can get a drink, a meal and also get pretty reliable news of what is going on in the rest of the world. It is also a meeting place and a good spot to make new friends.*[44]

On 24 February 1919, with his Russian pilot P Kravetz, Nunan was on a reconnaissance mission over the Onega region when their Sopwith 1½ Strutter was forced down over enemy territory. They were reported missing, and this information was relayed to his family in Blarney. For the following agonising two months, the family received no further information, but then in late April 1919, two months after being reported missing, it was confirmed that Lt Noel Daniel Nunan had been killed in action. It would appear that on the Sopwith being forced down, Nunan and Kravetz put up a fight, but Kravetz was killed outright, and Nunan was wounded and taken prisoner. Three days later, on 27th February 1919, Lt. Noel Daniel Nunan succumbed to his wounds and died as a prisoner of war.[45] He was "A" flight's first casualty, and his death cast a dark shadow over his fellow RAF officers. His body was never recovered, but he is commemorated on the Memorial at Archangel.

Aftermath

The Nunan family in Blarney was devastated by his death, and the local newspapers brought the story to the broader community.

ROLL OF HONOUR.

NUNAN—In North Russia, of wounds received in action on 24th February (previously reported missing), Lieutenant Noel Nunan, Croix de Guerre, R.A.F., second and dearly-beloved son of Dr and Mrs. Nunan, Woodville, Blarney, Co. Cork. R.I.P.

Irish Independent 25/4/1919 p.1   **Cork Examiner 26/4/1919 p.3**

As Noel had never married, his parents consulted a solicitor (Barry C Galvin, South Mall) to put his affairs in order. Coincidentally, Barry C Galvin's son, Barry St John Galvin, had also served in Russia with the NRRF and survived the experience. The patent for the Homestead near Grande Prairie was issued to the family, which was sold, and the proceeds sent on to his family. A grant of probate was issued in Cork; his assets amounted to £206.14.7, which was granted to his mother in May 1920. By the time the probate was granted, his father had passed away, and this is the reason that his mother was granted the proceeds.

His brother Alfred finished the war and returned to Canada, where he found work in the city of Vernon, British Columbia, working for the fruit growers O.W. Hembling, Contractors. When Alfred fell ill in 1961, he was hospitalised at the Colonel Belcher Hospital for Army veterans, which was opened in 1919 to cater for the large numbers of injured WW1 soldiers. Alfred John Nunan was just 66 years of age when he died in December 1961; he was afforded a military funeral service and is buried in Burnsland Cemetery in Calgary.

Burnsland Cemetery the last resting place of Alfred J Nunan (Gordon R. Penell)

As stated above, Noel's father, Frances, died in April 1920, and his mother, Annie Nunan, died in 1944 in Cork's Mercy Home at the age of 73. Two of his sisters (Frances Clare and Annie) emigrated to the US. His youngest brother, Clarance Raphael, qualified as a medical doctor and died in Banstead, Surrey, in 1974. Another brother, Henry Vincent, qualified as a dentist and practised in Midleton, Co Cork, until he died in 1945.

Noel Daniel Nunan is commemorated on the Archangel Memorial and remembered on page 596 of the Canadian First World War Book of Remembrance. In July 1919, the French president posthumously awarded Lt Noel Daniel Nunan the Croix de Guerre (with Palm) for services rendered during the Russian campaign.

1919 Canadian Book of Remembrance p.596

Croix de Guerre with palm

Meanwhile, the British newspapers reported and even exaggerated the severity of the heavy fighting on the river and railway fronts. Churchill and the War Office fed propaganda to the English newspapers to convince parliament that a relief force should be raised and sent out as soon as the spring thaw allowed.[46]

Chapter 8

Major Francis Mortimer Taylor, RAMC (Dublin)

Major FM Taylor (by kind permission of Patrick Groom)

Francis Mortimer Drake Taylor was born in Dublin in 1886 to Sir John and Lady Mary Taylor. His father was the Assistant Under-Secretary for Ireland based in Dublin Castle. The Taylors lived at 12 Bushy Park in Rathgar and had four children: Elizabeth Barbara, James Benjamin, Francis Mortimer, and Mary Claire. Francis, or Frank as he was known, was educated at the High School in Harcourt Street. Like his brother James, he trained to be a medical doctor, registering as a student in the Royal College of Surgeons (RCS) in 1907. Taking a break from his studies, Frank, in July 1909, travelled to New York to spend some time with his uncle Mortimer Keely in Brooklyn. He was described on the ship's passenger list as 5ft 5 with blonde hair, blue eyes and a tattoo of a 'dragon on right arm'. After seven years of study, Taylor graduated as a medical doctor from the College of Physicians of Ireland and Royal College of Surgeons in Ireland (LRCP & SI) in July 1914.

Frank and his brother James joined the Special Reserve of the Royal Army Medical Corp (RAMC) at the outbreak of the war. Following training, Frank was appointed Lieutenant on September 23rd, 1914. The RAMC, as well as providing front-line medical assistance, also set up and ran hospitals offering rehabilitation support for wounded soldiers. He was attached to the 45th Field Ambulance 15th (Scottish) Division and saw action in Flanders and France. Francis suffered from arthritis of the left hip from an injury he received in 1911 when a horse kicked him. This resulted in bouts of sciatica, from which he was hospitalised on several occasions during the war years. He requested and was granted a transfer to a warmer climate, and in February 1917, he set sail for Egypt. He was assigned to General Hospital No. 17 in Alexandria and transferred a month later to No. 36 Stationary Hospital in Mahemdia, Sinai. However, his sciatica returned, and in January 1918, he was invalided from Alexandria to Miss Birkett's Hospital in London for treatment. By July, he was deemed fit for 'General Service' and requested a transfer to the King's African Rifles as he felt the climate there would be more suitable for his arthritis. By the time his request was considered and granted, Captain Taylor had volunteered and been posted to the North Russian Expeditionary Force. His commanding officer informed the Colonial Office that he 'could not be spared'.[47]

Taylor was appointed Senior Medical Officer Vologda Force in the North Russian Expeditionary Force (NREF) from 1918 to 1919. Before he departed for Russia, Frank proposed to his sweetheart, Eileen Garvey, the daughter of surgeon Henry Garvey and his wife Alice, nee Birmingham. The couple then went to West & Son, the prestigious jewellers on Grafton St, and purchased a beautiful cluster engagement ring. They planned to get married as soon as he returned from Russia.

Taylor arrived in Archangel sometime in July 1918 as part of 'Elope' force, tasked with securing the port of Archangel and the railway link to Vologda. 'Elope' was split into the 'Dvina Force' for operations along the river and 'Vologda Force' to secure the railway. Taylor was attached to 'Vologda Force', which comprised British and American troops mainly based near the northern section of the Archangel to Vologda railway line, and their mission was to defend and hold the railway. In the following months, Taylor was busy treating casualties from the battles along the railway line and the many cases of frostbite as the winter began to take hold.

By this time (October 1918), Poole had returned to Britain, and Brigadier General Edmund Ironside had taken over command of the North Russian troops; he set about consolidating the front-line positions before the winter set when the rivers and seas would freeze solid. In the next few months, Taylor was involved in many battles along the Dvina, Vaga and Railway fronts as Ironside's plans were implemented for the winter. Ironside decided to push the Red Army back along the railway front and take and hold the towns of Kodish, Emtsa and Plesetskaya, as these could provide valuable bases for the expected siege during the winter months. The plan called for a surprise attack on the town of Kodish, which lay south of the Emtsa River, the town being held by a unit of the 6th Red Army, and then to push southwards and take the other two towns. But things didn't go as planned, and the British and American forces that were involved in the operation were pinned down by heavy machine-gun fire as they tried to enter the town of Kodish. In late December, the Allies attacked again, and a long-drawn-out battle resulted in many casualties before the town was finally taken. But while the Bolsheviks had been cleared from the town, they hadn't given up and continued to harass the troops who had taken Kodish and any reinforcements trying to reach the town (Sgt Kenney was killed in this battle).

Acting Major Frank Taylor distinguished himself during this operation and was awarded the Military Cross (MC) for his bravery and conspicuous gallantry under these trying conditions. The citation tells the story:

> *Awarded the Military Cross*
>
> *Capt. (Acting Major), Frank Mortimer Taylor, Royal Army Medical Corps, Special Reserve. For conspicuous gallantry and devotion to duty on December 30, 1918, at Kodish, when he urged his sleigh drivers into Kodish through severe fire. He thus established a dressing station, collecting and tending the wounded under difficult and dangerous conditions.*[48]

Following the failure of the Allies to extend the front beyond Kodish, they eventually re-established their winter base at the river Emtsa location where they had initially settled. After a quiet couple of months, things started to hot up again on the railway front, and Taylor was busy as he made his rounds visiting the various field hospitals and tending to the injured soldiers. Gunshot wounds and frostbite were the primary afflictions to be treated, and as the temperature again dropped, an increase in frostbitten hands and feet only added to his workload.[49]

On St Patrick's Day 1919, Major Taylor began his rounds, travelling to Obozerskaya and Bolshie Ozerki, which lay west of the railway line. Private Walter Stanley Roberts and 18-year-old Petr G. Federov, their sleigh driver, accompanied him. But they never reached their destination of Bolshie Ozerki and were reported missing. On the same day, several other troops went missing on the same stretch of road, and an investigation was initiated. On the 5th May, the War Office confirmed that Major Taylor, who was 'previously reported missing, now reported 5th May 1919, by the enemy as killed in action 17th March 1919'.[50]

The investigation continued, and in September 1919, the Sleigh driver Federov was located, brought to Archangel, and provided an account of what took place.

Inhabitant of Petrograd, Federov, Petr Gregoriavitch, aged 18 years, stated:

"In September, 1918, serving as seaman on the trawler 'Anthony', I arrived in Archangel. In October or November, I enlisted in the Slavo-British Legion and was attached to the transport as a driver. On March 23ʳᵈ, 1919 I was driving a British Doctor and Sergeant, whose names I do not know, from station Obozerskaya to the village of Bolshe Ozerki. Three versts from the village Bolshe Ozerki, about noon, we ran into a Bolshevik picquet. We were arrested and remained with the picquet, under guard. The picquet consisted of a Company of the Ryazan Soviet Regiment. About 11 p.m. the Company Commander ordered the Doctor and Sergeant, who were sitting with me by the fire, to rise and go into the woods. They obeyed. They were taken about 15 paces from the fire and shot there. Before being shot, they were undressed, and had only their underclothes on. The bodies were left and remained on the spot until the Company retreated on March 24ᵗʰ. After the execution, there was a quarrel among the Red Army men over the partition of money and rings, taken from the dead men. After the arrest, the Company Commander examined me and asked whom I was driving. I explained I was driving a Doctor and an assistant Doctor. Besides they might have known this, as red crosses were even on the uniform of the men shot.

(signed) Petr Federov
Correct (signed) Jadovski, Colonel
Archangel 8-9-1919 [51]

Federov claimed that the Bolsheviks told him he could leave and go home. When the Allies reached the location, they found the bodies of Taylor and Roberts, as Federov had indicated, and also the bodies of four other troops of the NREF, 2nd Lt Emanuel Leon Snyders, Private William Bell and drivers William Adams and Arthur Buckley, who had met the same fate. A full military funeral was afforded to the slain men, and they were buried in Bolshie Ozerki cemetery.

However, their graves are now lost to time, but they are commemorated on the Archangel Memorial.

Major Taylor, FM, MC, inscribed on the Archangel Memorial

Aftermath

Eileen Garvey never got over the loss of her fiancée and, for health reasons, decided on 17th December 1920 to return (she had worked there as a governess in 1915) to South Africa, where she died from TB in Bloemfontein in 1921.[52] The diamond cluster engagement ring that Frances bought her in Dublin remains within the extended Garvey family as a reminder of the 'betrothal of two young people in love'.[53]

When news of the tragedy reached his family in Dublin, the Taylors were heartbroken to lose their youngest son in such an isolated and desolate land. His father, Sir John Taylor, received a letter from the Director of Medical Services in North Russia stating that the deceased officer 'had displayed marked ability as an organiser in a most difficult area. He was very popular with all ranks and I feel his loss very keenly'.[54]

Things were also changing in Ireland as the popularity of the Republican cause was making life for British establishment personnel, such as the Taylors, very difficult. The stress of the political situation in Ireland and the tragedy of losing his son eventually took its toll on Sir John Taylor. Following a month's leave in April 1920, he was forced to retire and left Bushy Park and Dublin for good. Serendipitously, the next tenant at 12 Bushy Park was author, nationalist and friend of De Valera, Erskine Childers, who had landed guns from his yacht in Howth in 1914, who then opposed the Treaty and was executed in 1922 by the Irish Free State for possession of a gun and whose son, also Erskine Childers, would become Irish President in June 1973 and die in office less than six months later.

Sir John and his family returned to London and resided at Wissahickon, Sandy Lodge Rd., Hertfordshire, where their other son, James Benjamin, died of cancer in 1934. Their youngest child, Mary Claire, married Ernest Jensen in 1924, and they emigrated to the US, where Ernest worked in finance until he died in 1949. Mary Claire returned to Britain and eventually moved in with her parents and older sister, Elizabeth. Sir John James Taylor passed away in January 1945 at the age of 85, and his wife, Lady Mary, died 10 years later in 1955. Elizabeth, the eldest daughter of the Taylors, passed away in 1962, and the final surviving daughter, Mary Claire Jensen, died on 14th November 1970.

Major Francis Mortimer Taylor RAMC and 68 other pupils who perished in the Great War are commemorated on two brass plaques in the entrance hall of his alma mater, the High School, which is now located in Rathgar Dublin.

Major Taylor's death occurred more than four months after the Armistice, and many of the Allied forces were questioning the continued use of troops in Russian affairs. In late February 1919, the US Senate decided to end US involvement and pull its forces out of Russia as soon as possible. A few months later, Canada also decided to withdraw its troops from North Russia. The War Office in London now decided that the evacuation of all troops needed to occur within a timeframe that would see the last soldier leave Archangel before the freezing of the port in the winter of 1919. Churchill argued that in order to achieve an orderly withdrawal, more troops were needed on the ground. With only six or seven months to accomplish this orderly evacuation, the British government agreed with Churchill and set about raising two Battalions for the campaign. A call for trained volunteer soldiers was put out in newspaper advertisements throughout the UK on April 9th 1919, seeking volunteers for the North Russian Relief Force (NRRF).

Many of the volunteers were recently demobilised soldiers who were finding it difficult to find work in a world where trade had declined and Britain had imposed a 'contractionary monetary policy'. This strategy was a misguided effort to restore the gold standard to its pre-war status.[55] A second cohort of 'volunteers' came from those soldiers awaiting demobilisation, particularly Australian and Irish troops. Those serving troops who expressed an interest in joining the NRRF were demobilised to Class 'Z' (subject to recall) and immediately signed up for the duration of the North Russian campaign or one year's service, whichever was shortest. The pay was very generous by army standards, and each volunteer would be granted a two-month furlough with full pay and allowances on completion of the service. The NRRF also comprised some 'regular' troops ordered to be part of the relief force.

The two battalions were raised and readied within a few weeks for embarkation.

Chapter 9

Pte Michael (Hugh) McMillan, Machine Gun Corps
(Newtownards, Co Down)

Private Michael McMillan was a member of the North Russian Relief Force (NRRF) but was not a volunteer as his unit, the 8th Battalion Machine Gun Corps, was ordered to be part of Grogan's Brigade for North Russia. Following the call for 'volunteers' two Brigades comprising of about 5,000 men were made up of regular and volunteer soldiers. The first Brigade was to be commanded by Brigadier George William St. George, Grogan, VC, CB, CMG, DSO and became known as Grogan's Brigade, while the second Brigade was commanded by Lionel Warren de Vere Sadlier-Jackson CB, CMG, DSO and was known as the Sadlier-Jackson Brigade. Grogan's Brigade, made up mainly of regular soldiers, arrived in Archangel on 27th May 1919, while Sadlier-Jackson's Brigade, made up mainly of volunteers, didn't arrive until early June.

Hugh Keenan (why he put Michael on his army enlistment papers is a mystery – for the remainder of this story, the name Hugh will be used) McMillan was born on the 22nd of November 1894 in Newtownards, Co Down, to Andrew and Mary McMillan. He was the third son of the McMillan family, and they would go on to have one more son (Andrew) in 1900. Following the birth of Andrew, complications set in, and Mary passed away, leaving Andrew (Sn) to raise four young boys – James (12), William (10), Hugh (6) and baby Andrew. Andrew (Sn) moved his family to Belfast, where he would have help with the boys and where work was more plentiful.

When Hugh finished school, he found work as a Carman (driving a horse-drawn vehicle) for the local linen mills and worked there for several years, but when war broke out in 1914, he thought about enlisting, and in early 1915, at the age of 20 Hugh enlisted in the 1st Battalion of the Inniskilling Fusiliers. Following training, McMillan was assigned to the Machine Gun section; the Battalion moved to Rugby in Warwickshire to join the 87th Brigade, which was assigned to the 29th Division. In March 1915, the Division sailed for Gallipoli via Egypt and landed on the beaches around Cape Helles. Following an assault by the Royal Fusiliers, the 1st Battalion Inniskilling Fusiliers' mission was to consolidate the ground taken at X Beach, on the northwest side of the Cape, and await further orders. However, the delay extinguished the element of surprise and allowed the Turkish troops to mobilise and put up strong resistance to impede the Allies' advance. McMillan's Battalion spent several months making slight gains and repelling the Turkish forces' inevitable counter-attack. Before the year (1915) was out, McMillan had transferred from the 1st to the 6th Battalion Royal Inniskilling Fusiliers and then to the Machine Gun Corps as a horse transport driver and spent the next 3 years fighting in Gallipoli, Salonika, Palestine and Egypt.

In March 1919, McMillan found himself with the 8th Battalion of the Machine Gun Corps stationed at Dibgate, Shorncliffe. They then moved to Crowborough camp in Sussex and, in early May 1919, were informed that they had to prepare for service overseas as part of the North Russian Relief Force. On Monday, May 12th, they left Crowborough for Newcastle by train and set sail on HMS *Czarita* for North Russia the following day. They arrived in Murmansk on the 20th of May 1919 and proceeded to Archangel with the aid of ice-breakers one week later.

Colonel W. Marriott-Dodington, C.M.G., in charge of the 1st Battalion Oxfordshire and Buckinghamshire Light Infantry, recalled the welcome they received:

> *On 27th May the Brigade landed and was received by the Russian Authorities, Civil and Military. Our Commander (General Grogan)*

> *receiving the traditional offering of bread and salt, at a triumphal arch, erected in honour of the relieving troops.* [56]

The first two recorded deaths to occur within Grogan's Brigade were a suicide and a drowning. Lt Quartermaster George Dancy of the Oxford and Buckingham Light Infantry was found with a self-inflicted wound a few days after reaching Archangel. At the same time, Lance Corporal Alfred Phillipson of the Chesire Regiment drowned while swimming in the River Vaga on 11th June 1919. [57]

Following a couple of weeks of becoming acclimatised, the Brigade was moved by barge up the River Dvina and, on 5th June, reached Bereznik on the left bank of the Dvina River. Bereznik, lying about 170 miles from Archangel, was the headquarters for both the Dvina and Vaga riverfronts. The following day, McMillan's unit was assigned to two barges that proceeded down the river Vaga towards Kitsa and the enemy front.

The landscape in North Russia was comprised mainly of pine forests and swampy marsh ground. These conditions were not the best for transporting men and equipment to where they were needed. The Allies used the local drosky (a pony and small springless cart) to facilitate mobility to reach strategic parts of the dense forest. The drosky was used to pull guns and some of the heavier equipment, such as the miles and miles of line needed to keep communications open between the front troops and the command post in the rear directing artillery fire.

On the 16th of June, McMillan had his first brush with the Bolsheviks when his patrol came upon one of their camps, and a short battle ensued. The patrol killed several of the enemy before withdrawing without any casualties themselves. General Ironside, the Commander in Chief, visited the column headquarters at Ust Vaga, and it was decided to attack the enemy stronghold at Kitsa and Ignatovskaya on the 26/27 June in an attempt to push them back towards Shenkursk.

The plan, according to Marriot-Dodington, was:

...for the main column to move by the left bank, and after "mopping up", the enemy advanced position to capture Ignatovskaya. A small column was to move by the right bank and enter Kitsa after the capture of Ignatovskaya. The two columns would then unite, and after "mopping up" return to quarters'. [58]

Disaster struck when the leading column came under fire, and the pony with the communication equipment suddenly bolted, cutting the troops off from the rear command. However, they did manage to achieve their objective and captured the advanced position of the Reds without suffering any casualties.

McMillan's Machine Gun company was assigned to 'C' company of the Oxford and Buckinghamshire Light Infantry. Their mission was to attack along the Ignatovskaya Road. However, their progress was held up by an enemy blockhouse that the preliminary artillery shelling had failed to knock out. The platoon commander, Lt Norman Hughes, decided on a frontal assault on the blockhouse but became pinned down 50 yards from their goal.

Hughes was hit and badly wounded when the platoon got orders to withdraw as communication with headquarters was broken, and no reinforcements or artillery shelling could be requested. It was during this withdrawal that Private Hugh McMillan was killed by fire from the blockhouse. Several attempts were made to retrieve the fatalities and wounded (including Lt. Hughes), but it was an impossible task, and they had to be left on the field when the withdrawal took place. Eventually, the body of McMillan was recovered and buried in Ust Vaga cemetery a few days later. The casualties at the blockhouse were 2nd Lt Hughes and eight other ranks (including Private McMillan) killed, 30 wounded and five missing. The five missing soldiers were later ascertained to be prisoners of war and were released following the evacuation.

Hugh McMillan's body was recovered and buried in the nearby burial ground at Ust Vaga, which is now lost to time. His name is commemorated on a headstone (Sp.Mem. B.91) in the Allied Cemetery in Archangel.

AFTERMATH

McMillan bequeathed all of his property to his father, Andrew, when he made out his will in February 1917. His oldest brother, James, married Mary Adelaide Kelpie, had four children, and died in 1924. His father died in 1944, while his youngest brother married Hannah Beattie in 1923 and died in 1971. His remaining brother, William Scott, married Sarah Turner in 1918, had three children, and died in Belfast in 1972.

The families of the fallen were allowed to put a personal inscription on the headstone upon payment of a fee. When Hugh's family was asked if they wanted such an inscription, his father and brothers opted for the following: *GONE TO BE WITH CHRIST WHICH IS FAR BETTER.*

Chapter 10

Pte William O'Driscoll, 45th Battalion Royal Fusiliers
(Blarney Co. Cork)

Pte William O'Driscoll Royal Fusiliers

William O'Driscoll was born in Blarney Co Cork on 17th May 1899 to Mortimer Thomas and Margaret O'Driscoll; this would make him just 20 when he was killed in North Russia in 1919. Coincidentally, the registrar who recorded the birth, Frances Nunan, was the father of Noel Daniel Nunan (see chapter 6), who was killed in Russia in 1919. William was the 4th of 13 children to Mortimer and Margaret, who lived in a little house in the townland of Ardamadane in Blarney Co Cork.

Mortimer was a millhand in the local Blarney Mills, and as his sons and daughters reached 14 years of age, they followed their father into the local milling business. However, shortly after the outbreak of World War 1, William's brothers Mortimer (18) and John (19) decided to enlist in the British army. They enlisted in the Royal Garrison Artillery and were trained as gunners. After training, they left for the Western Front and disembarked in France in May 1915.

Meanwhile, back in Blarney, their father, Mortimer Thomas, at the age of 49, decided to enlist and joined the Royal Dublin Fusiliers. He must have lied about his age, as the army would only accept recruits up to the age of 45. An enlisting man did not have to produce evidence of age so that Mortimer Thomas would have been taken at his word regarding his age. Another of his sons, Richard, joined the Royal Munster Fusiliers. William couldn't wait to enlist, and as soon as he was 18 years of age, in May 1917, he reported to the enlistment office in Patrick Street and signed with the 4th Royal Irish Regiment, whose members at the time were stationed in Queenstown. The battalion travelled to England for training but was held in reserve and never reached the front lines before the armistice was signed in November 1918.

In the meantime, his brothers John, Mortimer, and Richard were experiencing life in the trenches and were involved in some serious battles. Mortimer suffered a shrapnel wound in August 1918, while John, around the same time, suffered from the effects of gas inhalation following a mustard gas attack. John managed a trip home around this time. He met with his brother William, and a photo of the two brothers in their army uniforms was taken.

William(RIR) and John O'Driscoll (RGA) in 1918 (Stephen Kelly)

The two insignia on William's left sleeve indicate a Marksman and Lewis gun training; thus, during training, he would have been skilled in the use of the Lewis gun, which had replaced the Vickers machine gun in 1916, and the crossed rifles badge would indicate proficiency in marksmanship. The sword that William is holding is probably his brother's, as Royal Irish Regiment soldiers would not have been issued with a sword.

Before the end of the war, their father, Mortimer Thomas, had transferred to the Labour Corps and, suffering from a severe case of arthritis, was eventually invalided out on health grounds with a pension. Still anxious for action, William, while awaiting demobilisation, heard about the recruitment for the Russian Relief Force and, after making enquiries, readily enlisted in the Royal Fusiliers in April 1919 and was sailing for Archangel the following month. After spending a week in Archangel, the brigade embarked on barges up the River Dvina to the front lines. General Ironside's orders now were to drive back the Red Army so that an orderly withdrawal could occur. O'Driscoll's battalion was stationed in the little village of Kourgomen on the left bank of the Dvina, just South of Troitsa, where the Bolsheviks were holding the line. On the morning of 30th June, O'Driscoll, with some of his comrades, was bathing in the river when he was carried away by the strong current. His body came ashore two days later, and he was buried with full military honours in the little cemetery in Kourgomen village. His name is commemorated on the Archangel Memorial. His mother Margaret was contacted with the tragic news, and she was awarded a 5/- shilling pension for the rest of her life. Several British soldiers drowned in North Russia owing to the fast-flowing currents in both the Dvina and Vaga rivers, which prompted GHQ to issue orders that swimming should only take place in organised 'bathing parties'. Nevertheless, drownings persisted up to the evacuation.[59]

Pte William O'Driscoll 45th Royal Fusiliers (133199) and formerly 4th Royal Irish Rifles (11936), interred in Kourgomen Cemetery and Commemorated on the Archangel Memorial (Sp.Mem. B.103).

Aftermath

The experiences of the O'Driscoll members who served in the Great War, brothers William (drowned), John (gassed), Mortimer (wounded), Richard (wounded), and father Mortimer Thomas (arthritis), didn't seem to put off the younger members of the family. In 1922, following the Irish Treaty, Morgan (20) and Walter (19) served with the Free State Army during the Irish Civil War.

John O'Driscoll, who had suffered from gassing in the war, continued to have pulmonary issues and, within two years of his demobilisation, had developed Tuberculosis (TB) and, on 3rd March 1921, succumbed to the disease. He was buried in the nearby Garycloyne cemetery. His father, Mortimer Thomas, died in 1928 from rheumatoid arthritis and was buried with his son John in Garycloyne. The marker on the grave was made from wood, and within a few years, it deteriorated and needed replacement. John's mother, Margaret, decided to write to the British Commonwealth War Graves Commission (CWGC) [60] and request a headstone to mark the grave where her husband and son were buried.

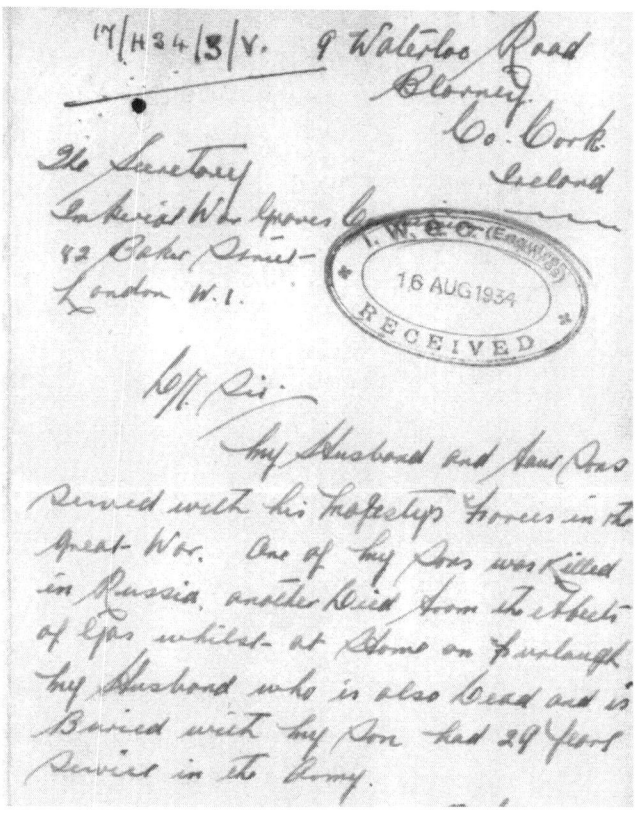

A portion of the letter sent to the CWGC by Margaret O'Driscoll

The letter stated the following:

9 Waterloo Road,

 Blarney

 Co Cork

 Ireland

 Dear Sir,

 My husband and four sons served with his Majesty's forces in the Great War. One of my sons was killed in Russia, another died from the effects of gas while at home on furlough. My husband who is also dead, and is buried with my son, had 29 years' service in the army. The object of this communication is to ascertain if the War Commission are the people who are responsible for the erection of a stone to the memory of my husband and son. In many of the cemeteries in Cork I have seen stones erected to fallen soldiers who served in the Great War and quite naturally I thought my deceased husband and son were entitled to a stone record erected to their memory.

 I would be grateful if you would furnish me with particulars as to how, and by whom, those headstones are being erected and if I am entitled to one.

 Thanking you

 & Beg to Remain,

 Yours Faithfully

 Margaret O'Driscoll

 August 14th 1934.

Two weeks later, Margaret O'Driscoll received a letter confirming that the CWGC would erect a headstone in memory of her son John, as he had died before August 1921, which was considered the official end date of the war.

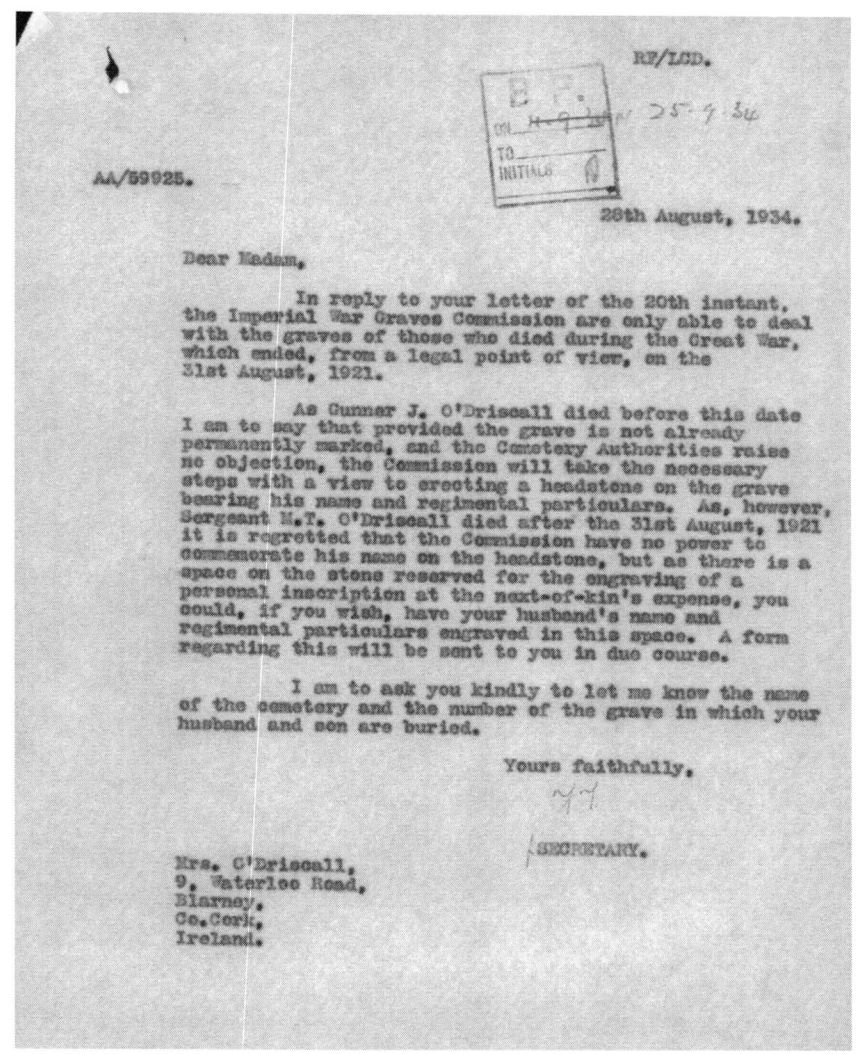

RE/LCD.

AA/59925.

28th August, 1934.

Dear Madam,

In reply to your letter of the 20th instant, the Imperial War Graves Commission are only able to deal with the graves of those who died during the Great War, which ended, from a legal point of view, on the 31st August, 1921.

As Gunner J. O'Driscoll died before this date I am to say that provided the grave is not already permanently marked, and the Cemetery Authorities raise no objection, the Commission will take the necessary steps with a view to erecting a headstone on the grave bearing his name and regimental particulars. As, however, Sergeant M.T. O'Driscoll died after the 31st August, 1921 it is regretted that the Commission have no power to commemorate his name on the headstone, but as there is a space on the stone reserved for the engraving of a personal inscription at the next-of-kin's expense, you could, if you wish, have your husband's name and regimental particulars engraved in this space. A form regarding this will be sent to you in due course.

I am to ask you kindly to let me know the name of the cemetery and the number of the grave in which your husband and son are buried.

Yours faithfully,

SECRETARY.

Mrs. O'Driscoll,
9, Waterloo Road,
Blarney,
Co.Cork,
Ireland.

It would take another 10 months before the stone was in place, as the CWGC, having agreed that John met the criteria for commemoration, then had to communicate with the Irish Board of Public Works, which was the body tasked with carrying out the work. Finally, in the summer of 1935, the headstone bearing the name of Gunner John O'Driscoll was erected.

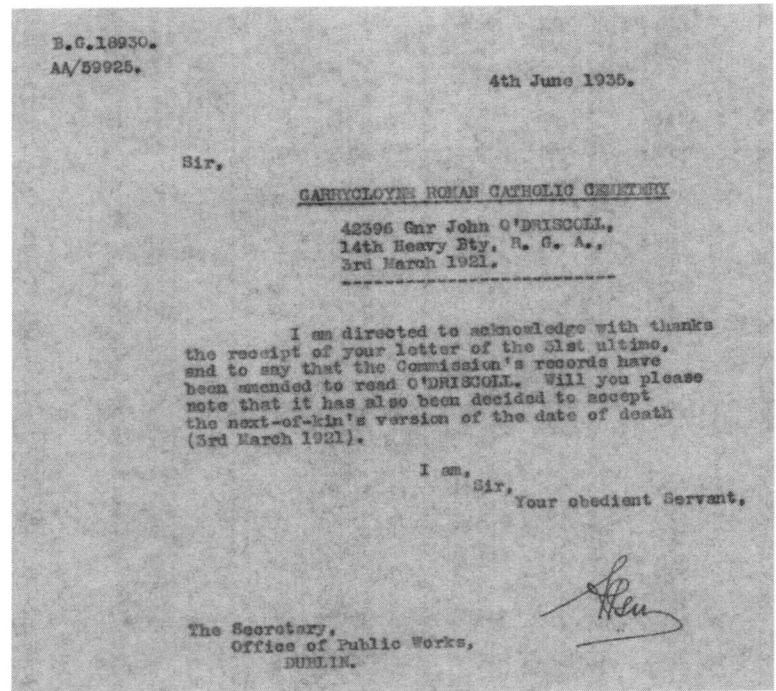

Letter June 4ᵗʰ 1935, from CWGC to the Irish Board of Public Works finalising the erection of a headstone to Gnr John O'Driscoll

But the O'Driscoll family were still not finished with war casualties, for on the 20th of November 1943, Walter, who had relocated with his wife to London, died while on official duty with the Home Guard in the Paddington area.

Walter suffered an injury while on duty with the 6ᵗʰ Middlesex Battalion of the Home Guard, and this injury caused infection (Bacillus Pyocyaneus), which developed into Meningitis. Walter was admitted to St Mary's Hospital in Paddington, where he died. Because Walter died whilst on duty, his family was allocated a CWGC headstone for his grave in South Ealing cemetery. Thus, the three O'Driscoll brothers, William, John, and Walter, are commemorated by the Commonwealth War Graves Commission in places as diverse as South Ealing, Garycloyne, and Archangel.

Top William is commemorated on the East Wall in Archangel, lower (L) John in Garycloyne, and (R) Walter in South Ealing

Chapter 11

Pte Patrick Hegarty, RAOC (Roscrea Co Tipperary)

By the time Private Patrick Hegarty arrived in Archangel in 1919, he had acquired quite a chequered relationship with the army. He seems to have enlisted four times in various units, was twice discharged as being unfit for service, spent numerous periods in detention for insubordination and deserted a few times into the bargain.

Patrick Hegarty was born on 3rd March 1892 to John and Maria (nee Melody) in Roscrea Co Tipperary. He was the fifth child of John and Maria, who would have four more children: five girls and four boys. His father, John, was a servant and gardener in the big houses around Roscrea and later Birr in King's County (now County Offaly). When Patrick was 17 years and 9 months old, he decided to join the Royal Irish Regiment (special reserves) and enlisted in Templemore. In August 1911, he transferred from the Special Reserves of the RIR to the Connaught Rangers. The following year, he was sentenced to 28 days detention for 'using insubordinate language', and in 1912, he was discharged from the army 'for misconduct' under paragraph 390 of the Kings Regulation and Orders for the Army. He was still under 20 years of age and, for the next two years, worked as a labourer for various farmers around the Roscrea area.

In March 1914, Patrick decided to rejoin the army. His brother James(born in Clonfert Co Galway) was a long-time soldier and, at the time, was serving in India with the Leinster Regiment; James had been writing home about his experiences in the army and seemed to be doing well. Patrick decided to apply and was accepted in the Leinster Regiment to try and follow in his brother's footsteps; however, within a short time, Patrick was in trouble again. In less than three months following enlistment, Pat was sentenced to 3 days detention for being absent without leave from the Tattoo roll call and for using obscene language to an officer. The following week, he was again charged with being absent from the roll call and for being drunk, and for this offence, he was sentenced to 14 days of detention. Charges continued in the following months. In May 1915, Hegarty's platoon was selected for service on the western front in support of the 1st battalion of the Leinster Regiment, who were involved in the second battle of Ypres. This was good news for Patrick because his brother James was serving with that battalion, and he hadn't seen him for several years.

James was 10 years older than Pat and had advised Pat to enlist in the Leinster Regiment, guessing they would have a better chance of meeting up if both were in the same regiment. James also had some news; while he was on a short period of leave to Roscrea, he had proposed to his sweetheart, Sarah Kelly, and they had become engaged to be married. As stated above, James had joined the army long before the war had broken out and had seen service in India before being posted to the Western Front in September 1914 with the 2nd Battalion of the Leinster Regiment. James saw action on the Aisne heights, which involved fierce fighting where the Germans had dug in on the heights above the Aisne river. James then transferred to the 1st Battalion of the Leinsters, was promoted to Corporal, and was stationed near Hooge, about 4km from Ypres, when he heard that his brother Pat was among the reinforcements being sent their way. They must have been looking forward to meeting up, but alas, it wasn't to be as on the very day, 4th May 1915, that Patrick was leaving for the Western Front, his brother James was shot and died later from his wounds.

It's not clear that when Patrick landed in France, he was aware that his brother James had been killed. But it is certain that when he arrived in the trenches near Hooge a few days later, he would have been told the sad news. At the time (10th May 1915), the 1st Battalion of the Leinster was under pressure during the Battle of Second Ypres and was glad to be reinforced by a platoon of 100 men (which included Pat Hegarty). Hegarty was only there two days when he received a gunshot wound to his right leg that fractured his tibia; this necessitated being sent to a field ambulance and then back home for his wounds to be treated. This meant that he spent less than two weeks on the Western Front, and in this short period, he had lost his brother James and suffered a severe gunshot wound to his right leg.

Back home, Hegarty was again getting into trouble despite the severity of his injury. Desertion, insubordination, and drunkenness were the main charges made against him, and in May 1917, he was, for the second time, discharged from the army, being declared unfit to serve. His mother, Maria, suffered a brain haemorrhage and died in January 1918.

Finding it difficult to find work around Roscrea with a badly injured leg Patrick Hegarty decided in the summer of 1918 to try and enlist in the army again. Incredibly, Pat was once more accepted into the army this time as a private in the Labour Corps. After six months of service, he was demobilised again in early March 1919. Following his demobilisation, Patrick spent some time in London. While visiting the War Office in Whitehall concerning his pension, he saw an advertisement calling for volunteers for the North Russian Relief Force and decided to apply. Probably due to his long military service he was accepted in April 1919 as a private into the Royal Army Ordnance Corps (RAOC), Reg no. S/9485.

Within a week, he had departed from Tilbury docks and landed in Murmansk on 19th April 1919. He was to be part of General Maynard's summer offensive to capture Medvyeja-Gora and advance down the railway line. Hegarty was part of the Royal Rifle Corps and the Middlesex Regiment 'Special Companies', specifically and hastily formed for service in North Russia for a summer offensive.[61] The duties of the RAOC were to supply and maintain the munitions for these front-line troops whose mission was to push southwards and eliminate 'the pockets of Bolshevik resistance as they were encountered'.[62] Over the next three months, Hegarty was kept busy as this mission was carried out, but on 7th July 1919, Patrick Hegarty was involved in some sort of accident and died as a result. It is not possible at this point to determine what exactly happened to Private Hegarty as the death certificate states the cause of death as 'Accidentally Killed'. What is known is in June and July 1919, the British troops (the US and French troops had been withdrawn at this stage) were using a large number of 18-pounder guns to dislodge the Bolsheviks from their well-defended positions. Hegarty would have been busy preparing and repairing the arsenal being used, and many accidents, often fatal) occurred at such times.

Ordnance QF 18-pounder gun (public domain)

Following his death, Patrick Hegarty was buried at Maselskaya burial ground near the Murmansk railway line. This cemetery is now lost to time and his name is commemorated on the Archangel Memorial.

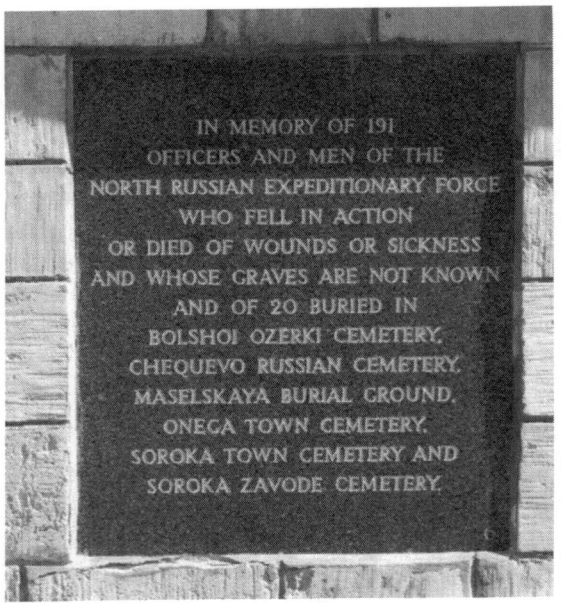

Pte Patrick Hegarty interred in Maselskaya burial ground (now lost to time) but commemorated on the Archangel Memorial

Aftermath

Patrick's father, John Hegarty, remarried in 1922 to Agnes Murray and settled in Birr Co Offaly. Later, in 1922, his father wrote to the war office and claimed the medals that were due to Patrick and his other son, James, who was killed on the Western Front in 1915. Both sets of medals were issued shortly after. While Patrick is commemorated on the Archangel Memorial (Stone no.10), his brother James Hegarty is remembered on the Ypres (Menin Gate) Memorial panel 44.

Chapter 12

Cpl Peter Mulhall, 45ᵗʰ Battalion Royal Fusiliers (Castlecomer, Co Kilkenny)

Peter Mulhall was born in Skehana, Castlecomer Co Kilkenny, on June 20ᵗʰ 1888, to John and Mary Mulhall. His father was a coal miner, a key economic activity in North Kilkenny since the mid-17th century. Peter was the second youngest of the eight children born in the Mulhall household. Of the seven surviving children, there were four boys and three girls, and as soon as the boys came into their mid-teens, they followed in their father's footsteps and took jobs in the coal mines, which had been in operation in Castlecomer for almost 300 years (the mines closed in 1969).

Coalmining didn't suit Peter, and in 1907, at the age of 19, he enlisted in the 2nd Battalion of the Leinster Regiment and shortly after was posted to Jullundar, Punjab, in India. After spending almost 4 years in India, Private Peter Mulhall must have enjoyed the experience as, in 1911, when his Battalion was due to leave India to be replaced by the 1st Battalion of the Leinster Regiment, who had arrived in Bareilly the previous month, Mulhall requested, and was granted, permission to remain there. He transferred to the 1ˢᵗ Leinsters and stayed in India until the outbreak of war in August 1914, when they were ordered to return to England via Bombay. They landed in Plymouth on 16 November 1914 and then moved to Morne Hill camp in Winchester, where they came under orders of the 82ⁿᵈ Brigade bound for France and Flanders. They landed in Le Havre for duties on the Western Front on 19ᵗʰ December 1914. In May 1915, while resting at Dickibusch on the Ypres salient in Flanders, the Germans made a surprise attack on the nearby St Eloi mound. The Germans took the mound and some nearby trenches, and the 1st Leinsters were ordered to retake the trenches and push the Germans back to their own lines, which they did, but not without heavy casualties. Luckily, Mulhall survived this battle unscathed and the 2nd battle of Ypres, where the Leinsters suffered many casualties.

In December 1915, the Battalion left the Western Front for Salonika as part of the Allies' war against the Bulgarian army on the Macedonian Front. They were involved in many significant battles in Salonika the following year, including the capture of Karajakois and Yenikoi and the unsuccessful raid on a Bulgarian outpost known as the Battle of Tumbitza Farm. Having transferred to the 29th Brigade, 10th (Irish) division, they moved to Egypt/Palestine in September 1917 to remove the Turks from that area. This was a much quieter operation, and in December 1917, Mulhall was allowed home leave and returned to Ireland.

While at home in Castlecomer, Peter Mulhall married Kate Dowling in St Patrick's Church, Clogh, Co Kilkenny. Kate's father, Thomas, also worked in the mines with Peter's father and his brother, Laurence. Peter also learned about his other brother's adventures. Michael had enlisted in 1915 in the Royal Irish Regiment, and he, too, was posted to the Western Front and experienced the harshness of life in the trenches.

The honeymoon was short-lived, as Peter had to return to the front early in the New Year 1918. He survived the war and, before he was demobilised, decided on one final adventure with the North Russian Relief Force. He signed up with the 46th Battalion of the Royal Fusiliers in May 1919, was promoted to Corporal, and posted to Lt Maxwell Perry's platoon that sailed from Leith on the SS *Steigerwald* on 3rd July 1919. Arriving in Archangel on 12th July, Mulhall was posted to VP455 on the Archangel/Vologda railway front near Obozerskaya.

Just when Mulhall's unit arrived at the railway front, the British learned of a Bolshevik plan to knock out the railway blockhouses. Their main objective was to take Obozerskaya at all costs, no matter what sacrifices.[63]

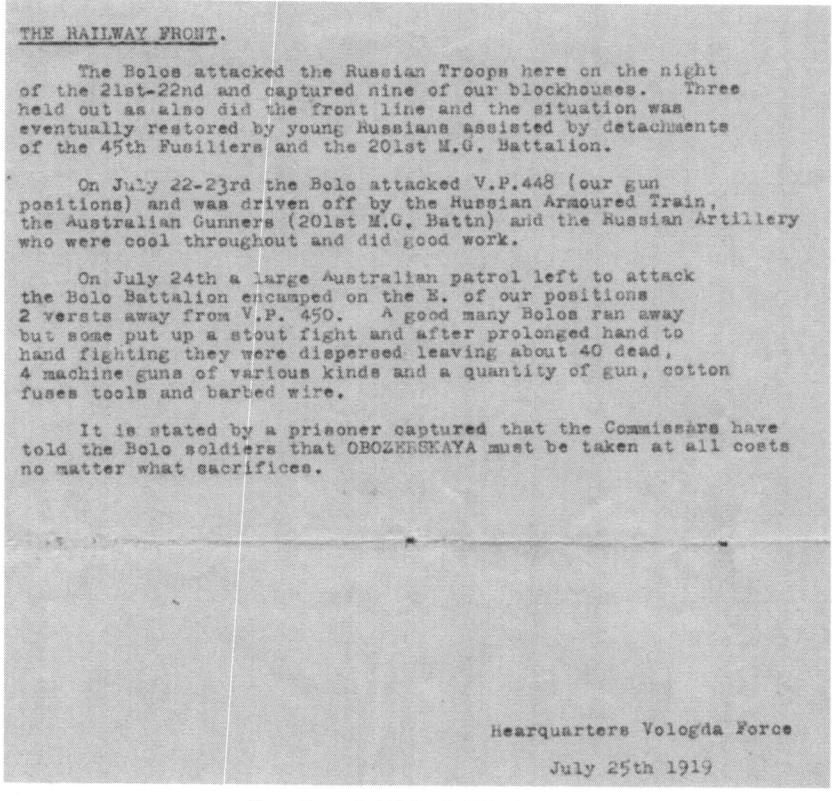

THE RAILWAY FRONT.

The Bolos attacked the Russian Troops here on the night of the 21st-22nd and captured nine of our blockhouses. Three held out as also did the front line and the situation was eventually restored by young Russians assisted by detachments of the 45th Fusiliers and the 201st M.G. Battalion.

On July 22-23rd the Bolo attacked V.P.448 (our gun positions) and was driven off by the Russian Armoured Train, the Australian Gunners (201st M.G. Battn) and the Russian Artillery who were cool throughout and did good work.

On July 24th a large Australian patrol left to attack the Bolo Battalion encamped on the E. of our positions 2 versts away from V.P. 450. A good many Bolos ran away but some put up a stout fight and after prolonged hand to hand fighting they were dispersed leaving about 40 dead, 4 machine guns of various kinds and a quantity of gun, cotton fuses tools and barbed wire.

It is stated by a prisoner captured that the Commissars have told the Bolo soldiers that OBOZERSKAYA must be taken at all costs no matter what sacrifices.

Hearquarters Vologda Force

July 25th 1919

Page from 2nd Brigade War Diaries

The attack duly occurred, and six blockhouses were captured by the Bolsheviks, along with some damage to the railway line, which hindered the movement of the British reinforcements. It was while defending VP455 that Cpl Peter Mulhall was killed by enemy fire, and his body was brought back to Obozerskaya for burial. Just 15 days after arriving in Russia, Cpl Peter Mulhall was buried with full military honours in the small cemetery at Obozerskaya on the Archangel/Vologda railway front. Over time, this cemetery became lost to the elements, and today, he is commemorated in the Allied Cemetery in Archangel.

Aftermath

After only two years of marriage, Kate Mulhall (only 19 at the time) got the shocking news that Peter was killed in North Russia, but the wider Mulhall family were a great support for her. Kate remarried Michael Pierce from nearby Coolcullen in 1921. Peter's brother Michael survived the war and was unsuccessful in his attempts to claim a pension from the British army. He claimed that he suffered from Malaria and Myalgia, but the Pension board found that his ailments were not 'due or aggravated' by his time in the army. Michael then returned to the coalmines in Castlecomer, but in 1939, at the age of 52, he got pneumonia and died.

Peter Mulhall is commemorated on special memorial B99 in the Commonwealth cemetery in Archangel Russia. He is commemorated in the Kilkenny World War 1 and World War 2 Memorials. According to *Ireland's Memorial Records, In Flander's Fields,* Peter Mulhall's place of birth is mistakenly given as 'Castleconner' instead of Castlecomer. This has resulted in Mulhall being commemorated on the Mayo Great War Memorial in Castlebar, as there is a Castleconner parish on the Mayo/Sligo border.

While it was thought that the cemetery at Obozerskaya, containing the remains of 27 Allied soldiers, was lost to time and the elements, more recent investigations have identified its location. The fascinating story behind this discovery will be dealt with in more detail in chapter twenty concerning the story of Private John Cairns.

Chapter 13

Pte Henry Frederick Begley, Connaught Rangers (Dublin)

Henry Begley Connaught Rangers

Henry Begley, the son of a Royal Irish Constabulary (RIC) constable, was 22 when WW1 broke out in August 1914, and he didn't hesitate to sign up with the Connaught Rangers. He was Attested in Maryboro, London, on 15th August 1914 and then posted to Crosshaven. The Rangers had been sent to Crosshaven to safeguard the entrance to Cork Harbour at the outset of the war.

Henry was the son of William and Agnes Begley from Birr in Kings County (Offaly). He had three brothers and three sisters. Because of the father's occupation (RIC), the family moved frequently, serving in places such as Parsonstown (Birr) in Kings County, Banagher in Kings

County, and Inishlaunaght in Co Tipperary before finally moving to Dublin when William retired from the RIC.

His older brother William also enlisted in the Connaught Rangers and was posted to Kinsale. Following his training in Crosshaven and Cork, Henry embarked for France in September 1914 and experienced trench life for the first time. During the second battle of Ypres, Begley was hit by shrapnel behind his left ear and was treated at a field hospital before being transported to the stationary hospital in Rouen, awaiting a ship to England for further treatment. Following his treatment in England, Henry returned to the front lines in France and spent the next few weeks in and out of the trenches.

In September 1915, his battalion was sent to Gallipoli in Turkey to participate in the Dardanelles' campaign just as he got news from home that his brother William was getting married in Dublin to his childhood sweetheart Josie McEvoy. Immediately on disembarkation in Turkey, Henry contracted a severe bout of Malaria and dysentery, which was to plague him for the duration of the war.

Following his hospitalisation, Begley returned to the Connaught Rangers in October 1915 and was posted to Salonica in Greece. Shortly after arriving, they were ordered north to support the Serbian army on the verge of collapse in their war with Bulgaria. Crossing the border into Serbia, Begley's battalion, the 5th Connaught Rangers, together with other battalions, were given the task of defending the Brigade's line along the Kosturino Ridge and Rocky Peak that the Bulgarians were attempting to take.

The fiercest hostilities occurred in December when the Bulgarians launched their main assault on the Ridge. The attack was so intense that the Connaught Rangers were forced to retreat:

> *'0500 Bulgars attacked Rocky Peak in great force with blowing of trumpets and beating of drums, and captured the position at 05.20,*

Captain Guine bringing the remainder of C Company and supports off in good order to foot of hill.' [64]

Fortunately, the Bulgarians didn't follow up on this success, and the British were able to create new lines of defence with the help of the French, who had been in Serbia before the arrival of the British. Following the disastrous battle of Kosturino, the British withdrew to Salonica, where the allies threw up a ring of barbed wire around the city, and a stalemate with the Bulgarians took place, with neither side able to make progress. This situation remained for the duration of the war, and because no leave was allowed, boredom became the norm for the soldiers stationed there. Begley's battalion, 5th Connaught Rangers, remained in Salonica until 4th October 1917, when they embarked for Alexandria. Two attempts by the Allies to take Gaza and Barsheeba failed, so the plan was to increase the reserves for the third attempt. The third attempt was a huge success, and as well as taking Gaza and Barsheeba, the Allies had also taken Jerusalem by Christmas 1917. Bouts of malaria and dysentery kept Private Begley out of action quite a lot, and one bout was so severe that he was sent to a convalescent hospital in Malta called Ghain Tuffieha.

Following his convalescence, Begley was returned to the field, but having completed their task in Egypt; the battalion was once again on the move – but this time back to France and the Western Front in an attempt to counter the Kaiserschlacht or 'Spring Offensive' begun by the Central Powers. It was now May 1918, and the previous month, the Germans had begun a series of attacks along the Western Front in an attempt to break the stalemate of the trenches before the Americans had time to mobilise and move their troops to France. While the Germans did make initial progress, they soon became entrenched again. When the Allies counter-attacked with the support of the Americans, the war came to a final conclusion in favour of the Allies.

With the signing of the Armistice the troops celebrated and soon were awaiting a troop ship home to 'Blighty'. Henry Begley was now 28 years of age. When he landed at Dover in April 1919, the Connaught Rangers actively sought men to attach themselves to the 2nd Hampshire Regiment for operations to relieve the British troops who had spent the winter in North Russia. The Hampshires were commanded by Lt. Col. Jack Sherwood Kelly VC, CMG, DSO, a battle-hardened soldier who had won the Victoria Cross on the Western Front in November 1917 for 'conspicuous bravery'. Sherwood Kelly was a charismatic figure, and when the call went out for volunteers to bring the 2nd battalion of the Hampshires up to strength, many men from various regiments (Somerset LI, Dorset regiment and the Connaught Rangers) answered the call.

Thirty-nine (including Begley) of the Connaught Rangers 'volunteered' for the operation. On 13th May 1919, following two weeks of training in Crowbridge barracks in Kent, they embarked from Tilbury on the SS *Stephen* for North Russia. Arriving in Archangel on 27th May, having stopped off in Murmansk, the troops were given a warm welcome from the anti-Bolshevik inhabitants of Archangel, and shortly after arriving, Begley and the 2nd Hampshires were travelling on barges up the River Dvina to Bereznik. Begley had his first taste of fighting the Bolsheviks when his battalion was ordered into the surrounding forests for a reconnaissance patrol. Three Red Army soldiers were killed in the battle, and Sherwood Kelly was commended by General Grogan:

> *The GOC wishes personally to thank you on the very gallant way you led the patrol on June 13th, 1919 which resulted in you killing three of the enemy at great personal risk to yourself. The information obtained by you was very valuable and the result of your encounter cannot but increase the morale of our men.*[65]

This would be the last time Sherwood Kelly would get a positive commendation from his superiors as he was to leave North Russia in disgrace within 2 months (more on that later). A plan was drawn up to support one of the Russian battalions (3rd Russian Rifles) to launch an attack along the front lines on the Dvina and take the towns of Topsa and Troitsa. The White Russians would attack Topsa directly while Sherwood Kelly's Hampshire troops would trek through the heavy swampy undergrowth of the forest and attack Troitsa from the rear and then link up with the Russian Rifles. While the Russian frontal assault was a complete success, the Hampshires found things difficult. Running low on ammunition, Sherwood Kelly withdrew, fearing they were being surrounded. Openly critical of 'those damn people who sit on their ruddy backsides behind and run the show'[66] Sherwood Kelly became a marked man for such views, but General Ironside decided to give him a 'second chance'.

Following several mutinies and defections among the White Russian troops, Sherwood Kelly became disillusioned about the role of the British in North Russia, which he articulated in several intercepted letters that would lead to him being relieved of his command and sent home. Before these dramatic events, two companies from the 2nd Hampshire were deployed to the railway front to support the Russians holding the line against the Reds. Private Henry Begley was a member of 'Z' company that made the journey from the Dvina to guard the railway front at Verst Post 445 (Verst Posts were railway markings 1 verst = .66 of a mile) near the village of Obozerskaya. Begley's company was billeted in some nearby blockhouses when not at the front line guarding the railway line.

Shortly after arriving at the Railway Front, a steady artillery barrage was aimed at the Hampshires. Unfortunately for Begley, on 27th July, just over two months after having arrived in Russia, his blockhouse was demolished with a direct hit, which killed him instantly. The following day, Private Henry Begley was given a full military funeral and buried in Obozerskaya burial ground. Because this cemetery was considered lost to time and the elements, Begley's name is commemorated on the Archangel Memorial, together with another 221 casualties killed in North Russia.

Aftermath

When Lt Colonel Jack Sherwood Kelly left Russia in disgrace, he decided to go public. He wrote to the Daily Express criticising British policy in North Russia and, in particular, Churchill's use of the Relief Force 'for offensive purposes on a large scale and far into the interior, in furtherance of some ambitious plan of the campaign'. Churchill went public and questioned Sherwood Kelly's loyalty and patriotism. The response was a second letter to the Daily Express in which Sherwood Kelly demanded a 'Court Martial'. Jack finally got his way, and on 28th October 1919, he found himself before a Court Martial at Middlesex Guildhall. The findings of the Court Martial gave Jack a 'severe reprimand', and two weeks later, he retired from the army, retaining the rank of Lt Colonel. Following unsuccessful attempts at a political career in 1924/25, Sherwood-Kelly travelled extensively in South America and Africa, where he contracted malaria, from which he died in 1931. Despite his earlier court-martial, Sherwood-Kelly was granted a full military funeral and is buried in Brookwood cemetery in Surrey.

Henry Begley's family were heartbroken when they received the news of his death, and his sister Lillian wrote to the British Army in late November 1919 to see if any personal items had survived from his time in Russia.

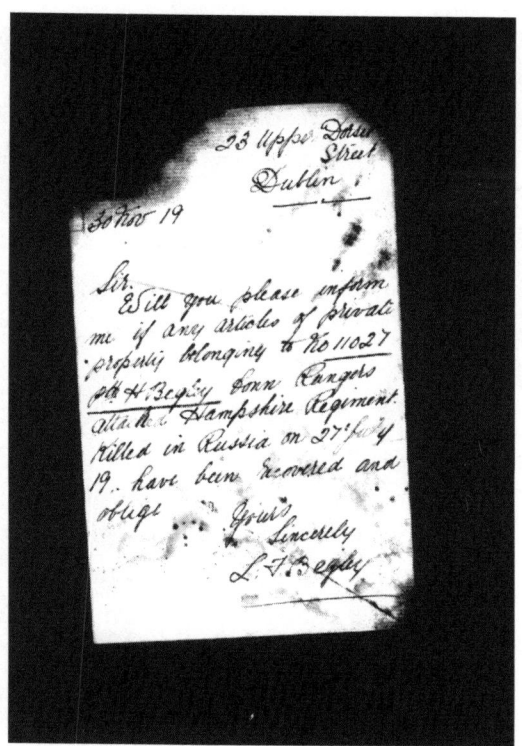

The letter reads:

23 Upper Dorset Street Dublin

30th Nov 19

Sir,

Will you please inform me if any articles of private property belonging to No 11027 Pte H Begley Conn Rangers attached Hampshire Regiment. Killed in Russia on 27th July 19., have been recovered and oblige.

Yours Sincerely,

L F Begley

Unfortunately, no items of a private nature were uncovered, and apart from his medal entitlements (his family received the Victory and

British War medals in 1921 and the 1914/15 star in 1924), nothing else was discovered to comfort his family. Henry's father, William, died in an early hospice known as the 'Rest for the Dying' located in Camdon St., north Dublin, in 1930. Lillian (Elizabeth Frances) was the only one of the Begley children to remain in Ireland; she married James Richardson, a clerk of works at Trinity College Dublin, and died in 1962.

His brother William survived the war and lived in Dublin with his wife Josephine; they had four children (David, Rhona, Lillian and William), and the family emigrated from Cobh to New York on the SS Republic in 1927. He worked as an electrician, and they settled in Detroit, Michigan, to raise their family. William died in Michigan in 1967. The oldest of the Begley children, Emma, emigrated to the US in 1906, married Richard Browne, had seven children and died in Minnesota in 1968. Another brother, Robert Vanston Begley, emigrated to the US in 1914, married, worked as a bank manager in Orange County, California and died there in 1956.

As previously stated, the location of the small cemetery at Obozerskaya has recently been rediscovered. The story behind this find, and the story of Private John Cairns will be elaborated on in chapter twenty.

Chapter 14

Pte Thomas Sharples, RAOC (Ballymoney, Co Antrim)

This soldier was the most difficult to research, and up to now, it has not been possible to determine whether he was Irish or not, but as he declared himself born in Ireland on his service papers, this is the reason for his inclusion.

The first record that could be found for Thomas Sharples is when he enlisted in the 4th Battalion of the Royal Inniskilling Fusiliers at Ludden Camp, Buncrana, Ireland, on 23rd February 1916. The three years between his enlistment and death on 5th August 1919 were the most eventful and complex of all the soldiers mentioned in this story. Private Thomas Sharples was lucky that he was not executed for the series of escapades that saw him being court-martialled three times on the Western Front.

Thomas Sharples enlisted in the British Army on 23rd February 1916 in the 4th Battalion of the Inniskilling Fusiliers, based in Ludden camp, Buncrana, Co Donegal. Sharples gave his address as Ballymoney, Co Antrim. The 4th Inniskilling Battalion spent the next 15 months on the Inishowen peninsula, training and preparing for action on the Western front.

Sharples seemed disheartened by the lack of action and may have questioned the unit he chose for enlistment. When he saw an advertisement in the Belfast Newsletter seeking recruits for the Quarrying Company of the Royal Engineers (RE), he decided to desert the Inniskillings, move south, and enlist in the above Quarry company.

QUARRYING COMPANY ROYAL ENGINEERS

Men of the following Trades are urgently required
for the above:—

Carpenters, Clerks, Electricians, Steam Engine Drivers, Internal Combustion Engine Drivers, Fitters, Gas Fitters and Plumbers, Masons,

For full particulars as to Pay, &c.,

Apply nearest Recruiting Office.

Belfast Newsletter 11th May 1917 p.8

From Dublin, he made his way to the Curragh Camp, presented himself as Thomas Pilkington, and was accepted into 327 Quarrying Company of the RE. On June 1st, 1916, as Pioneer T Pilkington, he embarked for the Western Front and a day later landed in Le Harve, where his company, consisting of 4 officers, 241 men, and two horses, was moved to Beaulieu.

Less than a month after landing in France, Sharples was arrested and held on suspicion of desertion. He then managed to escape from close arrest in Marquis, and the next we hear of him is when he presented himself to the 16th Infantry Base Depot at Etables and confessed to being Private Sharples, who deserted from the Inniskilling's back in May 1917. The offence was considered serious, and he was tried under a FGCM (field general court martial), found guilty and sentenced to 42 days of Field Punishment number 2. This meant that Sharples was not imprisoned but was placed in fetters and handcuffs and allowed to march with his unit, which by then was the 7/8 battalion of the Inniskilling Fusiliers. On the 2nd December 1917, Sharples was deemed unfit for active service and assigned to 862 Employment Company in Calais classified 'P.B.' (Permanent Base), meaning he should be kept on base duties permanently.

Less than two weeks later, Sharples again absented himself from his unit and 4 days later was arrested at Amiens but gave his name as Thomas Pilkington and was charged with deserting from 327 Quarrying Company back in June 1916. He was tried as Pilkington (his service in the Inniskilling's was unknown at this time) and released to resume service with his company. On 11th May 1918, he again absented himself from 327 company and reported back to 862 Employment Company as Private Sharples, where he was again arrested and detained for desertion. It was only now that the various links between Sharples and Pilkington were made, and Sharples was admitted to 30 General Hospital in Calais, suffering from mental exhaustion. He was released from the hospital in June 1918 and placed under close arrest, awaiting 'further evidence'. The following month (July 1918), Sharples was tried and confessed (see below) to fraudulent enlistment. The charge was 'dispensed', and Sharples was freed to serve the remainder of the war with the 862nd Labour Corps.

The next we hear of Private Sharples is in April 1919 when he 'volunteered' for the North Russian Relief Force (NRRF) and enlisted as a private in the Royal Army Ordinance Corps (RAOC). He was part of the 2nd Brigade (known as the Sadlier-Jackson Brigade), which consisted of volunteers who enlisted to … *serve His Majesty as a Soldier in the Regular Forces for one year provided your services are no longer required for the Special Service for which you have been enlisted, you will be discharged with all convenient speed* (Army Form B250A Short Service).

Two separate operations were taking place in North Russia—the Archangel offensive under Major General William Ironside and the Murmansk operation under Major General Charles Maynard. The decision to withdraw all allied troops by the end of the year had been taken, and the NRRF was raised to make this withdrawal as smooth as possible.

```
(a.) For Murmansk.—
     Railway troops, 2 companies and details* ...    ...    ...    ...    ...    ...    ...    720
     Royal Engineers –
         1 works company*        ...    ...    ...    ...    ...    ...    ...    ...    ...    150
         Signals*    ...    ...    ...    ...    ...    ...    ...    ...    ...    ...    240
         Electric lighting* ...   ...    ...    ...    ...    ...    ...    ...    ...    ...    40
     Royal Army Service Corps, Royal Army Ordnance Department, Royal Army    258
         Medical Corps.*
                                                                                      1,408*
     2 companies pioneers (unless provided by Allied troops as suggested in paragraph 3    400
         of this paper).
     Required to complete the present establishment ...    ...    ...    ...    ...    ...    587
                                                                                      2,395
                    Of these the most urgent are those marked thus : *.
```

Estimation of troops needed for orderly withdrawal from Murmansk (War Office, 1920:22)

Sadlier-Jackson's Brigade arrived in Murmansk on 3rd June 1919. While the majority of the Brigade left for Archangel three days later, a small number of the troops remained in Murmansk to help with the railway offensive about to take place. Sharples was among the contingent of soldiers that stayed in Murmansk, and a few weeks after his arrival, he found himself south along the Murmansk Petrograd railway, fighting the Bolsheviks. The RAOC was both a supply and repair corps. This meant that Sharples and his fellow RAOC troops had responsibilities for weapons, mortars and other military equipment as the offensive took place. It could be dangerous as it often meant working near the front lines in a mortar supply role.

On 4th August 1919, Private Thomas Sharples and his comrade Lance Corporal Peter Marshall were hit and seriously injured. Marshall (27), who was from the small town of Tillicoultry, Clackmannanshire, in Scotland, died a few hours later, and Sharples (48) died the following day. Both Sharples and Marshall were laid to rest, with full military honours, in the small cemetery near the town of Kem and wooden crosses were erected over their graves.

Final resting place of Pte Thomas Sharples and Lance Corporal Peter Marshall, Kem Cemetery, Murmansk (courtesy of IWM)

Their graves are now lost to time, but both men are commemorated on the memorial (Spec. Mem. B33) to the fallen in Murmansk New British cemetery, which, as stated previously, was erected in 1930.

Murmansk New British Cemetery

Postscript

As mentioned earlier, it is not possible to state definitively that Private Thomas Sharples was born in Ireland, although he claimed Ballymoney was his birthplace on his enlistment papers. While researching this soldier, the following information came to light that may indicate that Sharples was born in Ramsbottom, a small town in Lancashire, and, therefore, should not be included in this work at all. However, no link could be found between the Ramsbottom and Ballymoney Thomas Sharples, and consequently, it was decided to include him in this work.

Thomas Pilkington Sharples was born in Bury in 1871 to Thomas and Elizabeth Sharples; his father worked in the local Ironworks as a storekeeper. According to the 1881 census, the Sharples had three children: Thomas (9), Richard William (4), and Elizabeth Hannah (5 months). Once Thomas Pilkington Sharples hit his late teens, he began a life of criminality using different names at the times of the offences – aliases such as Goerge West and Thomas Pilkington. The offences he committed varied and included burglary, shopbreaking, crimes of a sexual nature, and military offences such as fraudulent enlistment. He did travel to Ireland in 1895 and was the subject of a court-martial in the Curragh Camp. By 1912, he had built up a lengthy criminal record, which the list below indicates.

| 23 | **Thomas Sharples**, 40, General Labourer.. 56 Days, Woolwich Court Martial, 1st Sept., 1892 (making false statement), as Thomas Pilkington. 28 Days, York Court Martial, 1st Apl., 1895 (making false statement), as Thomas Pilkington. 168 Hours, Curragh Camp Court Martial, 1st July, 1895 (breaking out), as Thomas Pilkington. 2 Yrs., Ashton-under-Lyne Court Martial, 24th July, 1896 (fraudulent enlistment), as Thomas Pilkington. 7 Days, Blackpool Police Ct., 7th July, 1899 (stealing a cap), as George West. 6 Mos., Liverpool Assizes, 14th Feb., 1903 (shopbreaking and larceny), as George West. 6 Mos., Edinburgh Police Ct., 5th Oct., 1903 (theft, 3 cases), as George West. 14 Days, Warrington Police Ct., 5th Dec., 1904 (stealing military canvas jacket). 3 Mos., Ambleside Police Ct., 20th Sept., 1905 (stealing a singlet), as George West. 6 Mos., Preston Sess., 27th Nov., 1907 (stealing an overcoat, &c.), as George West. 3 Mos., Runcorn Police Ct., 18th Feb., 1910 (stealing 4 pairs of stockings), as George West. 2 Mos., Penzance Police Ct., 6th Jan. 1911 (frequenting), as George West. | 5 | A. P. Brydson, Esq. ...... Ulverston. | 25th April |

Calander of Prisoners 1912: Thomas Sharples' list of past offences

Then, in October 1914, Sharples enlisted in the Duke of Wellington (West Riding) Regiment and deserted one week later. Interestingly, on his enlistment papers, he claimed to have previously served in the Dublin Fusiliers. His next of kin was given as Brother: Richard William Sharples, Station Master, Hellifield, Yorks. However, there is no solid link between the above Thomas Sharples and the Thomas Sharples that enlisted in Buncrana in 1916, so it is not possible to connect both men.

Interlude

At this juncture, it is time to reassess the situation in North Russia and the public unease in Britain about being involved in a war that seemed to have no rational explanation. As has already been stated, the Allies got involved in North Russia mainly to re-establish the Eastern Front following the Russian-German treaty of Brest-Litovsk and to safeguard the military stockpiles sent to Murmansk and Archangel. Following the armistice in November 1918 and the end of hostilities on the Western Front, the campaign in North Russia became more challenging to justify, and the public, through a media campaign, began to agitate for the troops to return home.

We have also seen that in January 1919, the British Government decided and made public the plan to evacuate all troops from Russia before the end of the year. Making such a plan public meant that any withdrawal plans were fraught with danger, not only from the enemy – the Bolsheviks – but also from the White Russians, who now felt betrayed by the allies. Winston Churchill, Secretary of State for War at the time, was ordered to prepare for the evacuation. This he did by coming up with a plan to raise a special contingent to relieve the troops in Russia, deliver a series of attacks along the front lines to disrupt the Reds and allow an orderly withdrawal. He also hoped that striking a blow so severe to the Red Army might enable the disparate anti-Bolshevik groups to re-organise under the North Russian Provisional Government and challenge the supremacy of Lenin's rule in Russia.

RELIEF FORCE FOR RUSSIA

THE RELIEF FORCE which is being formed for Service in North Russia will include the following: R.F.A., R.E. (Field, Signals, Postal), Infantry, M.G.C., R.A.S.C., R.A.M.C., R.A.O.C., R.A.V.C., A.P.C.

WHO MAY JOIN

The Force will be mainly composed of VOLUNTEERS drawn from the sources mentioned below :—

(a) Demobilised and discharged trained soldiers.
(b) Trained duration of the war soldiers serving at home.
(c) Soldiers at home serving on normal engagements or for 2, 3, or 4 years.

All men re-enlisting must be :—

(a) Fully trained in the Arm which they desire to join.
(b) Fit for General Service.
(c) 19 years of age and over.

A discharged or demobilised soldier, if accepted, will rejoin in the rank, substantive or acting, he held at the time he left the Colours.

PAY AND ALLOWANCES

PAY, ALLOWANCES and BONUS as now given to Men in the Armies of Occupation.

On completion of the period of service all men will be given two months' furlough or any longer period to which they may be entitled on full pay and allowances.

PERIOD OF SERVICE

The period of enlistment for recruits will be one year, or such shorter period as may be required, but no man who re-enlists for this duty will be kept longer than required for this special service.

The Advertisement calling for volunteers for the NRRF was placed in British newspapers throughout the UK

Thus, the North Russian Relief Force (NRRF) was established, comprising two Brigades totalling 8,000 troops. One would consist of 'volunteers' from the regular army, and the other would consist of volunteer ex-servicemen. Brigadier George Grogan would command the first Brigade, which was made up of regular troops under orders to serve in the NRRF. This was contrary to the Government's announcements that only 'volunteers were being sent' to North Russia.[67] The second brigade under Brigadier Lionel Sadlier-Jackson was comprised of volunteers – many who were awaiting demobilisation and would be discharged to 'Class Z' (subject to recall) and then enlist with the NRRF. Two units, the 45th and 46th (service) Battalions of the Royal Fusiliers, were formed in London in April 1919 specifically for duties in North Russia. They went for final training in Sandling Camp, Kent and were presented with their colours by General Lord Henry Rawlinson, Commander-in-Chief of the North Russian Expeditionary Force.

As stated, the NRRF landed in Murmansk and Archangel in June 1919 and quickly became enmeshed in holding the lines against the Bolsheviks. Churchill's hopes of uniting the various white Russians under a single banner began to fade as many of them mutinied and joined the Red Army. The strategy for the orderly withdrawal now began to take shape.

The Campaign on the Dvina Front: 10th August 1919

The plan was to initiate a surprise attack on the front line of the River Dvina and push the Bolsheviks from their entrenched positions. It was believed that the disruption to the Bolshevik forces would allow the British army to conduct a smooth withdrawal along the Dvina back to Archangel, where they would embark for Britain. For this operation, the 45th and 46th Regiments of the Royal Fusiliers were to be employed, and noon on the 10th of August 1919 was the designated start time. This wasn't as easy as it sounds, as the enemy was well embedded in the villages along both banks of the Dvina and was supported by reinforced blockhouses, which meant a frontal assault would prove costly and may not even succeed. It was decided to do a deep flanking movement on each river bank and attack the Bolsheviks in a land attack.

Several villages on each side of the river were identified and targeted as objectives to be taken by the initial attack. The three towns on the western bank, Selmenga, Gorodok, and Borok, were to be outflanked, attacked, and taken by the 46th Battalion Royal Fusiliers, while the three targets on the eastern bank, Seltso, Lipovets/Sludka, and Chudinova, were to be subject to the same operations and would be the target for the 45th Battalion.

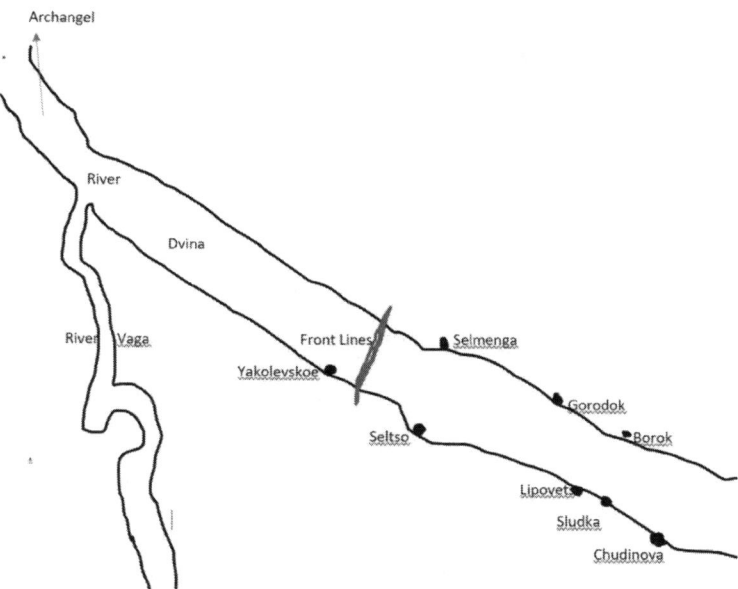

River Dvina front lines August 1919

Each battalion was to be further divided into three columns, with the objective of taking one of the designated areas on the Dvina that was subject to the assault. All the columns assembled in Yakolevskoe and set off on the outflanking movement, each breaking away to traverse the forest to its designated target.[68]

All the targets were eventually taken, and the operation was considered a significant success, but not without heavy casualties. It was estimated that the Red Army lost 500 men killed and over 2,000 taken as prisoners during this one-day offensive. British troops suffered their worst single-day loss in the North Russian campaign, with 38 killed and over 100 wounded. Four of those killed were Irish-born, and the following four chapters give more details about these deaths.

Chapter 15

Pte Edward Gallagher, 45th Battalion Royal Fusiliers (Cork)

Pte Edward Gallagher 7th Bt. South Lancashire Regiment (Author's Collection)

Edward Gallagher was born in Duncan Street (today known as Grattan Street) in the heart of Cork City in December 1882. His father, Michael, was a mason and came from a long line of masons that originated in Donegal, but eventually, some of that clan made their way south to Cork in search of work. When Eddie was 13, he went to work with his father and learned the trade of a mason. In 1907, he met and married Ellen O'Regan, a flax weaver in the Cork Spinning and Weaving Company located at Millfield on the north side of Cork City. He was a 'good catch' as he worked full-time on a well-paying job at the Queenstown (now

The call from John Redmond made up a lot of young men's minds (Public Domain)

The pay for a British soldier in 1914 was 7s (€0.40) per week, out of which he was required to give his wife an allotment of 3/6, to which the army would add 9s for his wife and 2/6 for each of his children. Overall, this would see Private Edward Gallagher receive 3/6 (€0.20) while his wife Ellen would receive the princely sum of £1 per week. This seemed an attractive arrangement, and together with the adventure and travel that awaited a man who had never journeyed outside of his native county, it must have seemed like an offer he couldn't refuse. Jack Savage advised Eddie to bring his birth and marriage cert with him to speed up the enlisting process, and on Monday, 16th November 1914, he collected them from the North Cathedral and made his way to Patrick St to 'join the ranks'.

The 'enthusiastic' recruitment officer was a member of the South Lancashire regiment and encouraged recruits to join it. Taking his advice, Eddie enlisted in the 7th Battalion of the South Lancashire Regiment of the British Army and was sent to Tidworth for training. Before he left, a photo was taken of Eddie in his recently acquired uniform.

Pte Edward Gallagher (12965) 7ᵗʰ Bt. South Lancashire Regiment (Auther's Collection)

The recruits were put through months of basic training around the open spaces of Salisbury Plain. The aim was to build up physical fitness and confidence, instil discipline and teach the military skills necessary for life in the front lines. In February 1915, they moved to Clevedon for brigade and divisional training; they then returned to Tidworth in March for some final trench training before embarkation. As the recruits were now almost 6 months in training, applications for 'home leave' were being accepted. Private Edward Gallagher (12965), 7th South Lancashire Regiment, was granted leave from April 20ᵗʰ to April 27ᵗʰ, 1915 and returned to Cork to see his family.

A great welcome from his wife, three children and extended family greeted Eddie as he made his way home to 5 Kerry Hall Tce, Gerald Griffin Ave. One of the first things Eddie wanted to do was get a photo of Ellen and the three children to carry them with him when he embarked for the front. With this in mind, on the first morning, they headed to Guys Photographic Studio on 70 Patrick Street, dressed in their finest clothes, where Ellen (34), Kate (6), Denis (5) and Elsie (4) posed for the portrait (below) to be taken.

Denis (5), Ellen, Elsie (4) and Kate Gallagher (6) in April 1915 (Author's collection)

All too soon, the 'leave' was over, and as Edward was travelling back from Dublin, the family went to the railway station to see him off. It was a sad occasion as no one was sure they would ever see Eddie again. Returning to Tidworth and some further training, Eddie finally embarked for France, landing at Boulogne on July 18th, 1915. Before leaving, Eddie got some good news from home: his wife Ellen was expecting their fourth child, due in January 1916.

The 7th Battalion of the South Lancashire Regiment was part of the 56th Brigade in the 19th (Western) Division, and their first significant action was the Battle of Loos in September 1915. Eddie's regiment was involved in a diversionary action at Pietre, the most significant British attack on German lines since the start of the war. It was also the first time that the British used poison gas, and no training could have prepared Eddie for the horror of what took place. But worse was to follow as his regiment was involved in many of the infamous battles in the war, including Albert (first Somme 1916), Ypres, Messines, etc. In April 1916, Eddie was sent to the field ambulance as a result of a gas attack but recovered quickly and re-joined his unit. However, there was one piece of good news when Eddie got a letter from home to let him know that he was now the proud father of a new baby girl, Mary (Maureen), born on 19th January 1916. The thoughts of seeing his wife and children again kept him going in the dark days ahead when he took part in some of the fiercest battles of the Great War.

In July 1916, the 7th South Lancashire regiment was involved in the Battle of the Somme, the largest battle of the First World War on the Western Front. Eddie's battalion was involved in the attack on La Boisselle that took place on July 3rd, 1916; in the preceding two days, the British had suffered 11,000 casualties[70] in trying to take this small but strategic French village. The difficulty was that the aerial bombardment that preceded the attack had failed to knock out the German dugouts. When the South Lancashire troops attacked, they suffered very heavy casualties. But they won the day when the village was finally cleared at bayonet point at 3 p.m. on the following day (4th). Fortunately, Eddie Gallagher was not among the casualties this time.

It's essential to understand what life was like in the trenches of the Western Front. For a start, most of the time, troops were in reserve in the supply lines or training establishments behind the front-line trenches. They would then be rotated in their turn to relieve their front-line comrades in the trenches. The usual pattern for trench duty was to spend a third of the time in the front-line trench, a third in reserve and a third at rest. Eddie's unit spent the following number of months out of the trenches. In October, the 19th Division returned to the Somme area, and Eddie's battalion was involved in trench duties, which were extremely uncomfortable due to the winter setting in. General Jeffreys described the conditions as:

> ... *the worst I ever remember in the war. The shell-fire was continuous, the ground was a mass of slimy mud which was up to and sometimes above the men's knees. There were shell craters full of water in which a man could easily be drowned.*[71]

Eddie spent the next month in and out of the trenches until finally, in November 1916, he took part in a significant offensive known as the 'Battle of the Ancre'. The battle was to be the final attack of the Battle of the Somme, and the intention was to attack the enemy lines with five divisions and reduce the German salient between Thiepval and Serre. For one of the operations, Eddie's unit was selected as the attacking battalion that would advance up the Hansa Road towards the village of Grandcourt and capture the German trenches running in a south-easterly direction. At dawn on the morning of 18th November 1916, the attack began and was going well, but when they were about two hundred yards from their objective, the Germans pinned them down with heavy machine gun and artillery fire. It was here near Grandcourt village that Eddie was hit in the leg, but he still managed to carry on with the attack; despite the heavy casualties, the 7th South Lancashire Regiment reached and captured their objective and joined up with the 8th Gloucesters on their right.[72]

The wound that Eddie received was from enemy artillery fire, which was described as 'exceptionally active' during the battle. Treated in a nearby field hospital and then in a Casualty Clearing Station, Eddie was finally sent back to England to convalesce. Wounded and sick soldiers who could get out of bed were issued a blue invalid uniform, sometimes known as 'convalescent blues' or more popularly known as 'hospital blues'. Because the uniforms of many of the wounded returning from the Western Front were caked in mud and possibly lice-ridden, the 'Hospital Blues' helped prevent disease and infection. The blue uniform also helped to distinguish the 'ordinary' hospital cases from these returning wounded heroes. Often, to keep up morale, photos were taken of these soldiers and printed on postcards to send to their loved ones. The image below shows Private Gallagher in 'hospital blues'; the back indicates that he cut himself out of a group photo.

Eddie in his 'Hospital Blues'   Back of photo showing postcard design (author's collection)

He spent several weeks convalescing and even managed a seven-day home leave pass to see his youngest daughter, Maureen, for the first time, who was nearing her first birthday.

After recovering fully, Private Edward Gallagher was returned to the front again. In the following year, the 19th (Western) Division, to which

Eddie's Battalion was attached, was involved in some of the bloodiest battles, including Menin Road and Passchendaele, which were part of the Third Battles of Ypres and also the Battle of Lys. However, there was a price to pay for those engagements, and the heavy casualties inflicted on the 7th S. Lancs. meant that they were forced to disband on 22nd February 1918; the 23 officers and 640 men (including Eddie) who survived the various battles were now sent to the 6th Entrenching Battalion. Until the end of the war, Eddie served with the 11th South Lancashire Regiment and the 1/5 South Lancashire Regiment, which was attached to the 170 Tunnelling Company.[73]

The work of the Tunnelling Company was to dig their way under the German fortifications and blow them up, but at this stage of the war, as the tide began to turn and the Allies advanced, the 170 Tunnelling Company worked on making safe and habitable the many villages, towns and facilities they captured. As Eddie was a mason, this was work to which he would be well suited and capable of completing successfully. One of the final operations Eddie was involved with on the Western Front was dealing with a huge fire in the village of Bethune.

Finally, on the 11th hour of the 11th day of the 11th month in 1918, the armistice was signed, and the soldiers on the Western Front were going home! To have survived the entirety of the war was no mean feat for Eddie Gallagher, as roughly 20 million people died in the 4 years, 14 weeks and 2 days of the war. Many of his friends and comrades would not be returning with him, and he looked forward to returning to civilian life and spending time with his wife and four children again.

Transported by ship from Calais to Dover Eddie Gallagher expected to be demobilised quickly and be on his way home to Cork. This was not to be! After being sent to several demobilisation dispersal camps, he eventually ended up at Crystal Palace awaiting final papers. And he waited, and waited, and waited! On the 9th of April, the Times newspaper carried a War Office recruiting appeal for volunteers to serve in North Russia. The advertisement was seeking *fully trained…fit…19 years or over'* soldiers to re-enlist for *'one year or such shorter period as may be required'* to relieve their British comrades who, it was claimed, were in a perilous situation in the frozen wastes of North Russia.

A few days before (5th), the same paper published a War Office statement about the critical situation in Murmansk and Archangel and how British forces were in grave danger. This story (untrue as it happens) was Churchill's way of preparing the British public for the prospect of sending more troops to Russia. Simultaneously, recruiting officers were dispatched to all barracks holding soldiers awaiting demobilisation and promises about repatriation, the granting of 2 months' furlough following service, and details of extra pay were all used as carrots to entice the battle-hardened troops to volunteer for one last mission. This might explain the strong Australian and Irish presence in the 45th and 46th Battalions of the Royal Fusiliers raised for this campaign. Escape from the boredom of camp life enticed Eddie and his mates to 'volunteer' for this adventure, so they were demobilised to Class 'Z' (subject to re-call-up) and then immediately re-joined the Royal Fusiliers.

Following his enlistment, Eddie was sent to Park Royal to train for the Arctic conditions they would encounter in North Russia. In early May 1919, the 45th Battalion Royal Fusiliers, consisting of 40 officers and 1000 men, were sent to Sandling camp near Shorncliffe for final training before embarkation. Following two weeks of drilling and training at Sandling, the troops entrained from Sandling railway station for Newcastle on 27th May 1919 and, the following day, boarded a ship bound for Archangel. After twelve days at sea, the SS *Oporto*, an old P & O liner with the 45th Royal Fusiliers on board, finally entered the port of Archangel. The green and gold church minarets may have reminded Eddie of another time and another world when he worked on the church spire in Cobh.

Two days after landing in North Russia, Eddie Gallagher and his battalion were shipped on three barges up the Dvina River to the front line, about 200 miles upriver. As the area is under the Arctic Circle, it meant having over 20 hours of daylight, which was a novelty for the soldiers. The most significant discomfort at this point was the number of mosquitos they encountered on the Dvina River; singleton-gates claimed that:

> ...*the whole Brigade fed the Russian mosquito as that insect had never before been fed. A mighty ukase must have gone forth to all mosquito tribes in North Russia, for the pestilent brutes attended the barges in their tens of thousands. Patent remedies and deterrents merely acted as choice cocktails.*[74]

Because of Kolchak's slow progress and several mutinies that had taken place in some of the Northern White Army Battalions, the original objective of reaching Kotlas became unattainable, and an orderly evacuation through the port of Archangel now became the main objective. The new plan called for the Red Army to be dealt a blow so severe that before he could recover and reorganise, all British personnel would be evacuated from North Russia. After two months of engaging in many skirmishes with the enemy, the day finally arrived, and the evacuation plan was to be initiated by a surprise attack on the Red Army. The plan called for an attack on both sides of the Dvina River, near the town of Troitsa, on August 10th at noon. This would allow the British to head back north to Archangel, where an orderly withdrawal could take place.

The 45th Royal Fusiliers were ordered to attack along the left bank and take the town of Seltso from the rear. Because the Red Army was entrenched around Seltso, it was decided to outflank the enemy, but this meant a three-day hike through heavy undergrowth prior to the attack. Consequently, on August 8th, at 18.00 hours, Eddie's battalion set off from Yakolevskoe for the gruelling hike through the forest, with hundreds of pack animals carrying the essential arms and ammunition for the surprise attack. Just after setting off, the rain started and continued for the next three days. The soldiers were issued machetes to help negotiate the thick vegetation underfoot. The conditions were dreadful, and the soldiers were exhausted as they had to carry full packs and slash their way through the dense undergrowth in heavy rain, turning the ground into a muddy quagmire. According to Singleton-Gates, the *...forest tracks were almost impassable. Most of the loads of the pack animals had to be man-handled for considerable distances.*[75]

The surprise attack was to take place at noon on August 10th. Because the 45th Royal Fusiliers were slowed down so much by the conditions, they had to keep going throughout the night of the 9th to ensure they reached their objective for the attack to occur successfully. Finally, they arrived deep behind enemy lines, exhausted but ready for the battle. For Sergeant Reg Mouat, a veteran of the Western Front who had been awarded the Military Medal for bravery in 1917, the conditions in North Russia were '*...hellish and worse than anything I met in France*'.[76]

The initial attack on the left bank began about 500 metres southeast of Seltso, and within a few minutes, the column Commander, Major Gerald de Mattos, was killed. Eddie Gallagher and his friends Jimmy Neill and Denis Mahoney had been assigned to a reserve platoon and were awaiting orders. The attack continued despite the heavy and accurate machine gun fire that was poured into the British troops from the Bolshevik forces, who were entrenched in blockhouses and other strategic positions. At around 12.30, having failed to break the Bolshevik defence lines, Eddie's reserve platoon was sent forward on the left flank. Due to the concentrated fire from the enemy, the reserve platoon was pinned down, and when the Reds counter-attacked, the situation became dire.

Following repeated attempts to break through, the Bolsheviks finally broke the Fusiliers' line and began to outflank them. It was here, about 500 metres from their objective at around 01.30 pm on August 10th, 1919, that a combination of Bolshevik shell and machine gun fire killed Private Edward Gallagher along with eleven of his comrades. The twelve brave soldiers were quickly buried in a makeshift grave by their comrades, and gathering up the many wounded, they hastily withdrew to the safety of their base in the forest.

The War Diary tells the story:

> *The pluck and endurance of the British Infantry was beyond all praise, the troops were without food for 24 hours before the attack… but despite this, and though dead tired, and soaking wet, the dash and spirit with which they attacked was beyond praise. The initial attack on Seltso failed owing to the strength of the position, the good defence put up by the enemy, and the failure of the Russian troops of this column.*[77]

Not all participants were so optimistic about the attack as Sgt Mouat described the scene as:

> *…a complete failure. No organisation as usual. The Captain had not the faintest idea what to do and nearly got us wiped out.*[78]

A second attack was more successful, and after twelve hours of fighting, the operation was a complete success. During this battle, three men fell into a swamp and were rescued by Australian Corporal A P Sullivan under heavy fire. For this act of bravery, Sullivan was awarded the Victoria Cross (VC). It was one of two VCs won by the 45th Battalion Royal Fusiliers in North Russia. A couple of weeks later, on August 29, fellow Australian Sgt. Samuel George Pearse displayed 'conspicuous gallantry' that was to result in the award of a posthumous VC.[79] Casualties among the 45th Royal Fusiliers amounted to about 150 officers and men killed, wounded or missing. At the same time, it was estimated that the Bolsheviks had about 3,700 of their 6,000 soldiers either killed or captured.

Before withdrawing from the field, Brigadier-General Sadlier-Jackson attended a burial and memorial service in nearby Yakolevskoe for the soldiers who had lost their lives in the Battle of Seltso.

Yakolevskoe Church ceremony for those who fell in battle August 1919 (Al Richardson)

These included the twelve soldiers who were hastily buried in the failed first battle: Lt GH Middleton R.A.M.C; Lt AV Colledge; Private W Hinson 130934; Private E Gallagher 129220; Private G Robinson 130256; Private P Gledhill 130269; Private FE Jones 130253; L/Cpl F Salisbury 131015; Private T Mclachlan 130143; Private J O'Neill 129217; Sgt J Bettany 128952 and Private WS Broadbent 129126 these twelve were commemorated on a memorial cross at Yakolevskoe church.

Temporary wooden cross for the 12 casualties of the Battle of Seltso whose bodies were never recovered (Al Richardson).

Two of the troops who died from their wounds (C Martin 129617 and J Bell 129796) were interred near the churchyard, where crosses were erected to mark the spot. Sadly, Edward Gallagher's body was never recovered from the temporary grave amid the dense undergrowth and forest where he fell.

The cross up close/ Pte E Gallagher's name visible in centre!

Aftermath

News of the tragedy arrived in Cork on August 30th with a standardised letter from the war office to Ellen Gallagher:

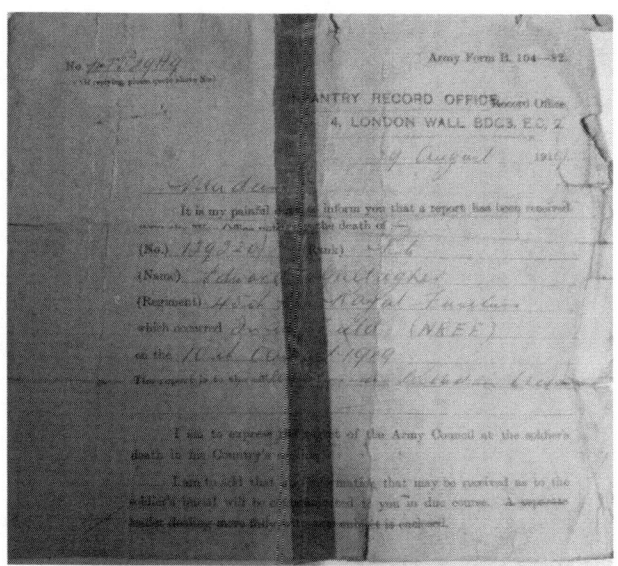

Infantry Record Office

4 London Wall Blds, EC 2

29th August 1919

Madam

It is my painful duty to inform you that a report has been received from the War Office notifying the death of 129220 Pte. Edward Gallagher 45th Bn Royal Fusiliers which occurred 'in the field' (NREF) on 10th August 1919.

I am to express the regret of the Army Council at the soldier's death in his country's service. I am to add that any information that may be received as to the soldier's burial will be communicated to you in due course.

I Am

Your Obedient Servant

The following week, a second letter arrived, this time from the Ministry of Pension, but this one was handwritten:

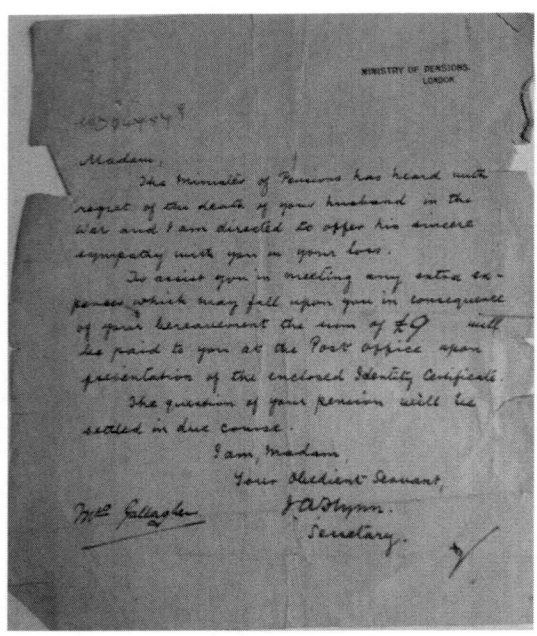

Madam,

The Ministry of Pensions has heard with regret the death of your husband in the war and I am directed to offer his sincere sympathy with you in your loss.

To assist you in meeting any extra expenses which may fall upon you in consequence of your bereavement the sum of £9 will be paid to you at the Post Office upon presentation of the enclosed identity certificate.

The question of your pension will be settled in due course.

I Am

Your Obedient Servant,

The medals Edward Gallagher was entitled to duly arrived from the Infantry Records Office in Hounslow on 23 June 1922. Because he had arrived in France early in 1915, he was awarded the 1914/15 star, which, together with the British War Medal and the Victory Medal, made up the trio of medals that became affectionately known by their nickname 'Pip, Squeak, and Wilfred'.

Eddie's medals, front and side view. The 14/15 star was given to soldiers who served in France from the beginning of the war! (Author's collection)

Following the battle of Troitsa (Seltso), the Bolsheviks were on the retreat, which allowed the British troops to pull back to Archangel, establishing defensive positions and planting mines on the River Dvina as they went.

The Archangel Allied Cemetery was begun immediately after the occupation of the town in August 1918 by the Allied forces sent initially to support Russia against any potential threat from German-occupied Finland and other local sources. The cemetery contains 224 burials and commemorations of the First World War, including special memorials to 140 officers and men with known burials in cemeteries elsewhere in northern Russia. Two of the burials are unidentified.

The Archangel Memorial, which consists of panels fixed into the east wall of the cemetery, commemorates 219 British officers and men who died during the North Russian campaign and whose graves are not known. Private Edward Gallagher is one of the men commemorated on the Archangel Memorial.

The author points out Eddie Gallagher's name on the memorial (Author's collection)

Eddie's widow, Ellen Gallagher, received a British pension for the rest of her life, and she lived with her daughter Kate (Kitty Twomey) in Old Friary Place off Shandon Street in Cork City until her death (aged 87) on 16th May 1969. Her daughter Maureen died on 25th March 1934 at the age of 17 from a heart condition, while her daughter Elsie

(Dennehy) also pre-deceased her when she died on 22 October 1968. Kitty died on 20th January 1978, and the final of the Gallagher children (Denis) died on August 8th, 1999.

Crosshaven 1962 with Ellen centre and daughters Kitty on left and Elsie on right (Author's collection)

Although she never spoke about him, it was clear that Ellen Gallagher missed Eddie in a big way. A box containing his medals, photographs, letters, and memorabilia was found among her possessions after she died, and these mementoes helped, in some small way, to bring his story to life.

Chapter 16

Pte Richard Power 45th Battalion Royal Fusiliers
(Dungarvan, Co Waterford)

Richard Power, born on July 4, 1901, in Dungarvan, Co Waterford, was the eldest of five children of John and Mary Power. The Powers were a poor family, and John, a labourer, found it hard to make a living in Dungarvan. All of the children, Richard, James, Roger, Jane, and Hugh, were born in the workhouse in Dungarvan, located west of the town, occupying a 5-acre site.

Young Richard was regaled by his maternal grandfather, Michael Walsh, a retired career soldier in the 61st (South Gloucestershire) Regiment of Foot, who had travelled the world with the army. Young Richard was fascinated with his grandfather's stories and promised to become a soldier as soon as possible. Grandfather Michael Walsh died in 1909, and young Richard was heartbroken. When World War 1 broke out in 1914, Richard couldn't wait to get in on the action.

In October 1916, when Richard was only 15, he went to the enlistment office in Lismore and, pretending he was over 18, joined the Dublin Fusiliers. His family did not know where he went, but it was not unusual for Richard to go missing. He was posted to Cork but, maybe because of his young age, had several minor infringements documented on his files, which included being 'dirty on parade' and 'absent for parade'. However, a year later, his actual age was discovered, and he was discharged from the army on 22 September 1917. Interestingly, his discharge papers recommended that he re-enlist the following year. In November 1918, he re-enlisted in the Dublin Fusiliers but was too late to see action on the Western front. When, in May 1919, the opportunity arose to volunteer for the Royal Fusiliers, being raised for the North Russian Relief Force, he duly enlisted. Richard may have continued to pretend he was older as the requirement for the Relief Force was that volunteers had to be '19 years of age or older' – Power was 2 months short of his 19th birthday.

Richard Power was killed during the second attack on Seltso; as this battle has already been described in the Edward Gallagher chapter, it suffices to say that Private Richard Power was one of three Irishmen to be killed in that battle (Gallagher, Neill, and Power).

Aftermath

Following his death, Richard's mother, Ann Power, living in Davis St., Dungarvan, was granted a pension of 6 shillings for life. Unfortunately, Ann Power only lived another year and died on June 2, 1921, from Meningitis in the Dungarvan workhouse.

Two of Richard's brothers, Hugh and Roger, emigrated to England in the 1930s. Both worked in the building trade. Hugh married Nora Scovell in 1939. They lived in Southampton, where he died in 1980. Roger died at the age of 56 in Winchester.

Private Richard Power is commemorated on Stone 5 in the Archangel cemetery, as his grave is lost to time. He is also remembered on the Waterford WW1 Memorial Wall.

Chapter 17

Pte Christopher Barry, 45th Battalion Royal Fusiliers
(Roscrea Co Tipperary)

Christopher Barry was born in Roscrea, Co Tipperary, on Christmas day 1898 to John and Mary Barry. At the time, the Barry family lived at Limerick Street, and Christy had an older sister, Mary, and an older brother, Richard. By the time of the 1911 Census, John and Ann had moved to Alleys Lane to accommodate their growing family, as they now had six children—the three younger than Christy were Jane, Kate and Annie. Christy's father worked as a nailer, but work was scarce, and it was hard with six children to make ends meet.

Christy Barry was a bit of a wild child and, aged 13, found himself in court on a larceny charge. It would appear that on November 12, 1912, Christy and his friend Patrick McGrath had stolen some cakes from the confectionary shop on Rosemary Street. While the cakes were missed, the lads seemed to have gotten away with it. Unfortunately, they returned to the crime scene the following day and tried to do the same again, but the proprietor, Blanche Benson, was more alert this time and called the police, and they were arrested. Because they were both underage, it meant that both fathers, John Barry and John McGrath, were also named as defendants in the case. Both parents were ordered to enter into recognisance in the sum of £1 condition on their sons keeping the peace and be of good behaviour for 12 months. They had to pay 1/- (one shilling) each towards the costs.

Summons against Christopher Barry and John Barry (Father) for the larceny of confectionary

Sometime during the summer of 1913, Christy and his older brother Richard got talking to their neighbour Robert Jolly, who was a 28-year-old soldier in the 6th Battalion of the Leinster regiment. Jolly was a well-known character around the streets of Roscrea; he had been arrested on numerous occasions, mainly for being drunk and disorderly and had even spent some time in prison for aiding the desertion of a fellow soldier by helping to dispose of his uniform. He joined the army in 1907 and regaled the young Barry brothers with the excitement of army life.

Jolly convinced Richard to enlist in the Leinster Regiment (which he did in November 1913) and for Christy to do the same when he reached the required age. Christy couldn't wait, and in August 1915, aged 17, he applied and was accepted into the 7th battalion of the Leinster Regiment. Sent to the Curragh for training, Christy spent any leave in Dublin, where he met Margaret Redmond, who lived in Palmerstown, and they quickly fell in love. Each time he was granted leave, he would return to Dublin and his sweetheart Margaret. Because Margaret's father, Myles Redmond, had been a soldier who fought in the Boer War, she was familiar with the idea that a soldier's life often meant him being away for long periods, which was also true for Christy's soldiering.

Following his training, Christy embarked for the Balkans in September 1915 and sailed for Greece to link up with his army comrades and mentor, Robert Jolly. The battalion was deployed to Salonika and fought various battles on the Macedonian front. On 6th December 1915, on the Salonika front lines, Christy and some of his comrades got lost and wandered into enemy lines. One of the group, Tim Farrell, was killed, and Christy, along with seven other troops, including Robert Jolly, were taken prisoner and transferred to a prisoner of war camp in Bulgaria. Christy celebrated his 18th birthday in the Bulgarian POW camp at Philippopolis, and the conditions there were horrific.

> *At the prison camp in Philippopolis, the troops were herded into filthy barracks in lots of one thousand. Many men chose to sleep outside rather than face the vermin at night. Their rations were totally inadequate and unpalatable.*[80]

Christy's family in Roscrea were contacted in January 1916 to say that Private Christopher Barry, 6th Battalion of the Leinster Regiment, was reported as missing in Macedonia. For two months, the family heard nothing, but then, on 14 May 1916, the family were relieved to hear that Christy was alive but being held as a POW in Bulgaria. He remained there for the duration of the war, and following the war's end, Christy returned to England, where he was listed on the weekly casualty list and admitted to hospital for treatment and convalescence.

He was allowed home leave in January 1919, and before he returned, he proposed to his sweetheart Margaret Redmond, who accepted his offer. They were married in the Church of the Nativity of the Blessed Virgin Mary in Chapelizod. All too soon, his leave time was over, and he returned to barrack life in England, leaving his young wife behind. Little did he know that this would be the last time Christy would see his beloved bride.

For the next two months, Christy Barry waited and waited to be demobilised and became bored with camp life. When he saw the call for 'volunteers' for the North Russian Relief Force, he jumped at the chance to see some action, and the promise of two months paid leave when they returned also influenced his decision. He duly was demobilised to Class Z, which meant he was subject to recall, and then he immediately, on 22nd April 1919, signed up for the Royal Fusiliers and was sent to

Sandling for final training and then sailed for Archangel on May 27th aboard the SS *Porto* with the rest of his comrades in the 45th Battalion Royal Fusiliers.

It should be remembered that Christy still hadn't celebrated his 21st birthday and had packed a lot of adventure into his short life. Here he was now, far from Roscrea, far from his young wife in Dublin, travelling on a barge up the Dvina away from Archangel, heading towards the frontline 200 miles upriver. Following the decision to withdraw from Russia, the British decided to push the Bolsheviks back down the Dvina and have an orderly, unimpeded withdrawal from Archangel. As stated earlier, the 10th of August was decided on as the date to spring a surprise attack on the Bolsheviks on both sides of the Dvina and deliver a 'blow' so severe that an orderly evacuation could take place.

The column was ordered to march on the left-hand bank through the forest and attack the towns of Seltso, Sludka-Lipovets and Chudinova from the rear. After a gruelling two-day march through the forest, Barry's column found themselves at the rear of Sludka-Lipovets, where they were ordered to stay hidden and await zero hour. The rest of the column advanced to their objective, the town of Seltso (Gallagher was in this column). Christy Barry's column began their attack on the small towns leading up to Sludka-Lipovets and, within two hours, had 'triumphantly entered Sludka'.[81] However, just as they entered the town, a shell directly hit the Column Headquarters, killing the commander, Major Stanley Le Fleming Shepherd and eight other ranks, including Private Christopher Barry. These casualties were given a full military funeral in the Yakovlevskoe cemetery.

A few weeks later, Christy's young wife Margaret learned of his death and was awarded a widow's gratuity of £5.0.0 and received a pension until her death.

Aftermath

Christy's brother, Richard Power, survived the war but did suffer a gunshot wound in April 1918. He continued soldiering after the war in the Royal Dublin Fusiliers. In January 1919, Richard married Mary Ann Griffin from Clontarf and settled in Dublin. Christy's sister, Annie, in 1934 married Thomas Arnold in Howth Co Dublin and died there in 1999. Christy's oldest sister Mary moved to Dublin and married Joseph Murray, and in 1935, while walking with two of her children on Coleraine Rd., Phibsboro, she was struck by a lorry that had collided with a car. While the two children were unharmed, Mary suffered catastrophic injuries and was rushed to the nearby Richmond hospital, where she was pronounced dead.

Private Christopher Barry is commemorated on Stone 4 in the Archangel cemetery, as his resting place is now lost to time.

Chapter 18

Pte James Neill, 45th Battalion Royal Fusiliers (Carlow)

James Neill was born in the Carlow workhouse to 18-year-old Eliza Neill on 15th April 1888. The workhouse in Carlow was located on Kilkenny Road and was opened in 1844 at a cost of over £10,000. Workhouses were institutions that provided shelter and food to those unable to support themselves financially and in dire need of help. The conditions in the workhouse were very severe, degrading, and stigmatising for the people who ended up there. This was particularly true for young girls who became pregnant and were often shunned by their families, their only option being to present themselves at the local workhouse (or poorhouse as it was known then). Hopefully, they would be allowed in to have their babies. Despite the hardship and stigma of life in the workhouse for pregnant, unmarried women, there was a widely held belief, particularly among the catholic clergy, that offering these very basic conditions to pregnant women might be encouraging 'immoral behaviour'. One local clergyman claimed that 'the shelter of the poorhouse is no doubt a great encouragement of this class (pregnant girls) as they are enabled by the law to come and go as they please'.[82]

No information about James' father is available, but 5 years later, Eliza found herself back in the workhouse giving birth to a daughter, Bridget. It must have been a very tough life for Eliza Neill, being a single parent of two children in Carlow and trying to make ends meet. James went to work at an early age working for a farmer, William Nolan, in Moyvally, Carlow. He worked on the Nolan farm for a few years, and then, in 1905, he decided to join the army. At the time, Dublin, Kildare, Wicklow and Carlow were fertile locations for Royal Dublin Fusilier enlistments, and army life must have been an attractive proposition for 17-year-old James to consider.

James enlisted in the Royal Dublin Fusiliers and was sent for training with the 2nd Battalion stationed at Buttevant. He was then transferred to St George's Barrack in Pembroke to link up with the 1st Battalion before they embarked for Malta. In November 1905, they were posted to Alexandria and then India, where they remained until the outbreak of war in August 1914. The battalion then returned to Britain, arriving in Plymouth in December 1914, and was sent to Torquay until March 1915, when they embarked for Gallipoli. They were involved in the 'V' beach landings in Cape Helles, where they suffered incredibly high casualties, losing almost two-thirds of their number in casualties in just two days of fighting.[83]

The Allied forces fought in Gallipoli for seven months, but the campaign was a total failure, and the British cabinet decided in December 1915 to withdraw all forces, apart from those at Helles, from the peninsula. On 1 January 1916, the Battalion was ordered off the Gallipoli peninsula and returned to Alexandria. In March, James was diagnosed with Bronchitis and, after treatment, was sent to the Mustapha Convalescent Hospital in Alexandria to recover.

The Battalion then moved to the Western Front and was involved in the first Battle of the Somme. In October 1917, James Neill was admitted to the 18 General Hospital in Camiers, suffering from venereal disease. He was treated and sent back to his unit. He was then reassigned to the 7th Royal Irish Regiment (18401) and finished the war with this regiment. Following the armistice, Neill resigned from RIR and enlisted in the 45th Battalion Royal Fusiliers for the campaign in North Russia.

Following a couple of months of training at Sandling camp near Folkestone, Private James Neill embarked from Newcastle for Archangel with the Royal Fusiliers on 28 May 1919. On 3 June, the SS Oporto, with James on board, arrived in Archangel, and the Royal Fusiliers prepared for the long trip up the Dvina River to relieve the troops on the front lines. As was already outlined (see Chapter 14), the plan was to mount a surprise attack on the Red Army, push them far back from the front lines, and organise an orderly withdrawal through the port of Archangel before the enemy could regroup.

August 10th 1919, was the date set for this 'surprise' attack, and members of the 45th Battalion Royal Fusiliers under the command of Major Gerald de Mattos were given the task of attacking and taking the Bolshevik position at Seltso on the western bank of the Dvina. As this battle has been covered in depth in chapter 14, it is sufficient to state that the British troops came under heavy fire as they approached Seltso, and it was here that Private James Neill was mortally wounded and died later in the evening of August 10th 1919.

Aftermath

James Neill was buried in the field, and as his grave is now lost to time, he is commemorated in the Archangel Cemetery on Stone no. 5 with others of his battalion. The War Office held a register of financial effects belonging to the next of kin of soldiers who died in the Great War. According to 'Soldier's Effects' for James Neill, the money calculated due to him in June 1920 was £6:7:3. This amount was awarded to his sister Bridget on 2nd June 1921.

He was eligible for the Campaign medals (the British War Medal, the Victory Medal, and the 1914 Star) duly sent to his last known address. His medals were returned under Kings Regulation 992, which meant that they were undeliverable (usually due to the family moving and no forwarding address available), they would be held for one year, and, if still unclaimed, would be returned to the War Office. James's medals were never claimed.

Nevertheless, there was some communication in September 1923 from James's sister, who gave her address as the County Home Carlow.

The County Home was on the site of the former Army Barracks and had been populated by the inmates of the Carlow workhouse when the Irish Army commandeered the workhouse site. Over 200 inmates were transferred on January 30th 1923, from the Workhouse on Kilkenny Road to the County Home on Dublin Road.[84] It must be assumed that Bridget remained an inmate of the workhouse since her mother's death in 1909 when she was just 6 years old. Now, aged 20, Bridget had applied for a pension from the British War Office. Bridget's application was successful, as she claimed to be financially dependent on James prior to his death. Bridget was awarded a small pension (not more than 16/6) and received this for the following number of years.

Chapter 19

Yeoman of Signals Patrick Casey, Royal Navy (Waterford)

Patrick Casey Royal Navy (Courtesy Yvonne Kennedy)

Patrick Casey was born in Waterford in 1886, and his family lived in Jail Street in the heart of the city. They were a well-to-do family, as his father, John, worked as a pig buyer and supplied many of the butcher shops in the area with the pork they needed. Patrick was the second youngest of six children and the youngest boy, having an older brother, Michael, who was two years older than Patrick.

After leaving school, Patrick worked with his father but didn't care much for the pig-buying business, and in July 1903, aged 17, he decided to go to England for a bit of adventure and find his way in life. His sister Ellen had emigrated to England several years previously and now was married to William Godwin and living in

Bristol. Patrick joined his sister in Bristol, and shortly after arriving, he decided to join the Royal Navy, but as he was under 18 years of age, he joined the Boy service of the Royal Navy. The following year, on 21st March 1904 (his 18th birthday), he signed up for a 12-year engagement with the Navy.

Patrick on the left with his brother Michael and father John Casey in 1911
(Yvonne Kennedy)

Patrick spent any leave due to him at his sisters in Bristol, and there he met Doris Godwin, a niece of his brother-in-law William. They quickly fell in love and were married on one of his shore leaves in March 1917. The following year, a baby boy, Patrick K, arrived, and the couple were over the moon, but it was a dangerous time for Patrick Sn as World War 1 was in full swing, and he served on several ships that saw plenty of action including HMS *Vernon*, HMS *Victory* and HMS *King George*.

Following the end of hostilities on the Western Front, Patrick Casey was transferred to the China gunboat HMS *Glowworm* for operations in North Russia. By late April (1919) the ice had melted, and the port of Archangel was again open. The main task of the ships and monitors in North Russia was to provide Naval gunfire support to the land forces attempting to push the Red Army back to facilitate an orderly retreat from Archangel. Following the sustained bombardment of the enemy lines on the Dvina riverfront, "*Glowworm*" and HMS *Cockchafer* were directed to steam downriver for some relief work. As the ships neared the village of Bereznik, one of the naval ratings on watch duty informed Commander Sebald W.B. Green about a barge on fire mid-stream dead ahead. Commander Green decided to go to the aid of the stricken vessel and gave the order for the fire station to assemble on the foredeck and prepare to extinguish the fire on the barge. The crew of the army barge had abandoned the ship as they knew something that Green didn't know – the barge was packed with live ammunition amounting to tonnes of high explosives.

When "Glowworm" approached the burning barge, many crew members, including Commander Green, gathered on the bridge and deck to watch the action below them. As they watched, a massive explosion occurred, resulting in a wall of flame lighting up the night sky and enveloping the deck and bridge of Glowworm. A second blast quickly followed this, and then a third that sent projectiles and missiles in all directions. Of the 54 crew members of Glowworm, 24 had been killed outright in the explosion, including Commander Green, 4 British Officers, 2 Russian Officers and 17 men. Unfortunately, Yeoman Patrick Casey, who had also made his way to the foredeck to watch the spectacle, was killed instantly by a flying projectile in the first explosion. Another four had been killed on a nearby barge, bringing the total killed to 28, and there were over 18 seriously injured.

THE CASUALTIES ON THE GLOWWORM.

The Secretary of the Admiralty issues the following :—

Information has been received from the Senior Naval Officer at Archangel that on the 27th August a fire occurred on board an ammunition lighter, and H.M.S. Glowworm and H.M.S. Cockchafer, not being aware of the contents of the lighter, closed to render assistance, when an explosion occurred, the Glowworm and Cockchafer being damaged, the former seriously. The ship, however, will be able to steam after repairs.

The following casualties are reported :—

Glowworm—Officers Killed—Temporary Lieutenant Thomas Lottimer MacFarlande, R.N.V.R.; Surgeon Lieutenant Richard Mortimer Rowland Thursfield, R.N. Died of Injuries —Acting Commander Sebald Walter Bluett Green, D.S.O., R.N.

Injured—Lieutenant Anthony Herbert Gerard Thorold, R.N.; Gunner Albert Milton Wildbore, R.N.

Men—Killed—Ayres, Joseph, Officer's Steward, 2nd Cl. (Po.); Casey, Patrick, Yeoman of Signals (Ch.); Cleveland, Robert George, Leading Seaman (Po.); Coase, Edward Henry, Able Seaman (Dover); Dawes, George, Leading Seaman (Po.); Farmer, Thomas William, Signalman (Ch.); Glanville, Leonard, Able Seaman (Ch.); Hill, Sidney, Able Seaman (Po.); Keith, Alexander, Leading Seaman (Ch.); Leadbetter, William George, Able Seaman (Po.); McCoy, John Robert, Able Seaman (Dover); McCrae, John, Stoker, 1st Class (Po.); Murray, Frederick, Able Seaman (Ch.); Smith, Lancelot William Henry, Able Seaman (Po.); Spellgrove, Ernest, Able Seaman (Dev.); Sykes, Harold, Armourer's Crew (Dev.); Wright, Henry, Able Seaman (Po.).

Irish Times 2nd September, 1919 p.5

Yeoman of Signals Patrick Casey was buried with full military honours in the Semenovka Cemetery near Bereznik. While this grave is now lost to time, he, along with his comrades who also perished, are commemorated on the Memorial in Archangel Allied Cemetery, Russian Federation. The following words of Rudyard Kipling are carved out on the memorial stone:

"THEIR GLORY SHALL NOT BE BLOTTED OUT" (Ecclesiastical 44.3).

Aftermath

In 1921, Patrick's widow Doris married her brother-in-law Michael J Casey, and they had one child (John) together. The two boys, Patrick Jr. and John grew up as brothers. In 1924, Michael J Casey, at 41, died in Bristol, leaving his wife, Lillian, a widow for the second time. Doris died in 1956 at Townlands Hospital, Henley-on-Thames.

Chapter 20

Pte Michael Mahoney RAMC (Cork)

Michael Mahoney, the son of a labourer, was born in Cork in 1880. He joined the army (Royal Garrison Artillery) when he was 18 and saw service in South Africa during the Boer War. On his return to Ireland, he relocated to Dublin and worked as a labourer. While in Dublin, he met Anne Elizabeth Murphy, who worked as an assistant in the Tea Trade, and they began to live together on Upper Wellington Street in the Rotunda area. When Annie became pregnant, they decided not to get married until after the baby was born. Mary was born on the 9th of May, 1905, and Annie and Michael were married the following month. Unfortunately, the child Mary was a sickly child and developed TB, which was rampant in Dublin at the time due to overcrowding, and she died in March 1906.

Even though Mahoney was 36 years of age when war broke out in 1914, he immediately enlisted in the Royal Army Medical Corp. The medical doctor's examination stated that 'teeth are of poor grade as he has only two upper teeth' but concluded that Mahoney 'is a fine type of man and fit for the duration of the war'. On 26th March 1915, Private Mahoney embarked for France but was immediately sent back to England, deemed 'medically unfit' due to the condition of his teeth. He seemed to have overcome the problems with his teeth as he returned to France in July 1915 and stayed there until December of the same year. His service records indicate that he was in quite a bit of trouble in the army, losing many days of pay for offences such as 'hesitating to obey order', 'absent from Roll Call', and 'Drunk in camp'. He was also sentenced to 3 stretches of Field Punishment no. 1, meaning he would be placed in restraints and attached to a fixed object such as a post or gun wheel for up to 2 hours per day.

On his final visit to the trenches, while serving with the Lincolnshire Regiment, he took part in the first attack on Bullecourt, which was part of the first Battle of the Scarpe. In the early months of 1917, under pressure from the Somme campaign, the Germans retreated to the Hindenburg line, and the Allies devised a plan to finally break through the German lines. It was agreed between the Allies that the French would make advances along the Aisne River and break through the Hindenburg line in mid-April 1917, but in a diversionary tactic, one week earlier, the British would start an offensive from Arras (50 miles north of Aisne) and weaken the German strength for the French assault on Aisne.[85]

As part of the Arras offensive, four Australian divisions of 1 ANZAC Corp were to attack Bullecourt. At the same time, the British (62nd Division) would attack further north and take Hendecourt before linking with the troops at Bullecourt. Mahoney was part of the 62nd Division and, in the early stages of the attack, was wounded in the left thigh and evacuated from the battlefield. The attack on Bullecourt was a complete failure, with over 3,000 casualties.

After treatment in a field hospital, Michael Mahoney was sent back to England on the hospital ship the *St Andrew*. The wound cleared up without complications, and in May 1917, Mahoney was allowed home to Dublin to visit his wife and their two children, Patrick (10) and Mary (9). Three of their children had died – Mary in 1905, aged 10 months; Arabella Margaret in 1913, aged 3 months; and James in 1915, aged 5. It must be stated that this high mortality rate was not unusual for those living in the slums of Dublin at the time, and 45 Upper Wellington Street, the home of the Mahoney family, was such a slum as it accommodated seven families comprised of 28 people who shared this modest-sized house with only one outside toilet.[86]

In January 1918, Mahoney was transferred to the 5th Training Battalion of the Royal Army Medical Corps in Blackpool and, in June of that year, was posted to the Curragh Army camp in Kildare. This meant that he could visit his family in Dublin more often. However, when the war finished, he returned to England (Blackpool), awaiting demobilisation. He was demobilised to class 'Z' in January 1919 and signed up for the North Russian Relief Force shortly after.

He arrived in Archangel in June 1919 and spent the next two months helping with the high volume of medical conditions in North Russia. In July 1919, Mahoney received a letter from his wife, Annie, saying that she had given birth to a son, whom she called James in memory of their son, who died in 1915.

In August 1919, Private Michael Mahoney took ill, and on 26th August 1919, he died – the post-mortem indicated that 'Edema of Glottis' was the cause of death. As the 'glottis' is part of the larynx, it is quite possible that the trouble that Mahoney had with his teeth in 1914 contributed to his death in 1919. He was buried in Ust-Pinega cemetery (Ust-Pinega cemetery holds three British graves: Driver Nathaniel F. Croucher, Engineer William Johnston and Private Michael Mahoney), which is now lost to time, but Private Michael Mahoney, Royal Army Medical Corps is commemorated on Special Memorial B94 in Archangel cemetery.

His wife Annie was awarded a pension and remained in 45 Upper Wellington Street for the remainder of her life. She died on 24th February 1942 at the age of 60.

Chapter 21

Pte John Cairns 46th Battalion Royal Fusiliers (Belfast)

John Cairns was born in Knockrullen, Strabane, on 8th July 1889 to John and Elizabeth (nee Patterson) Cairns. His father, John, was a general labourer, and the family moved to Belfast, where work prospects were more fruitful for labourers. John (jr) left school early and worked as a General Labourer, staying as a boarder in Annette St. in the Market area of Belfast. He met and married Elizabeth Cassidy in April 1911, and they went to live in Kingston Street, Belfast. The following year (1912), Elizabeth gave birth to a daughter, Elizabeth Patricia, and they were now living at Verner St in Belfast. Elizabeth Patricia was a sickly baby, and at 8 months of age, she succumbed to congestion in her lungs and died on 13 December 1912.

Like many men his age, John (24) enlisted and joined the 1st Battalion of the Queen's Own Cameron Highlanders when war broke out. Following training John embarked for France in October 1915 and experienced life in the trenches. Following a home leave in late 1916, Elizabeth found herself pregnant and, in July 1917, gave birth to a baby girl. They decided to call her Elizabeth Patricia after the child they lost in 1912. Cairns was involved in many of the main battles in France, including the Battle of Mons and the subsequent retreat, the Battle of the Marne, the Battle of the Aisne and the first Battle of Ypres. While the Camerons lost almost 6,000 men in the First World War, John Cairns survived the carnage.

Following the Armistice in November 1918, Cairns was 'cooling his heels' awaiting demobilisation. In April, he volunteered for the North Russian Relief Force, which was being mobilised in April/May 1919.

He enlisted and, within a month, was sailing from Leith on the SS *Steigerwald* heading for Archangel. He arrived in Archangel on 3rd July 1919 and was posted to Lt. Maxwell Perry's platoon of the 46th Battalion Royal Fusiliers on the Archangel-Vologda railway front at Verst Post 455.

Cairns was involved in one of the final battles on the railway front, attacking the Bolshevik battery position near Emtsa. This battle was requested by General Evgeni (Eugene) Miller, the General Officer Commanding the White Russian forces in North Russia, to General Henry Rawlinson, who had taken over command from General Ironside for the evacuation of North Russia. Miller wanted to improve the morale of his troops before the British withdrawal and believed that taking back control of Emtsa would provide the needed inspiration and motivation.

The plan was to trek through the forest and deliver a surprise attack on the Bolshevik position at 05.30 hours on the morning of 29th August 1919. Cairn's platoon was part of Major Harcourt's force that would attack the Bolsheviks from the right-hand side, while Major May's force would simultaneously attack from the left. The Bolsheviks were well protected by a series of blockhouses ringed by barbed wire that needed to be cut so the Fusiliers could knock out the guns in the blockhouses. Private William Baverstock of the 201st MGC described the attack on the blockhouses:

> *Captain Newbold leaped from behind a tree and with a yell, led his men forward to attack the Bolshevik position. Some Fusiliers were killed and wounded as they rushed from tree to tree, approaching the enemy.*[87]

It was while they were taking the final blockhouse that Private John Cairns was fatally wounded, and he, along with several of his fellow soldiers, was buried in Obozerskaya Burial Ground. A Celtic cross was erected to the memory of the soldiers killed in this battle (also buried in Obozerskaya burial ground were previously mentioned Private Henry

Begley and Cpl Henry Mulhall) for his part in the same operation, Sgt. Samuel George Pearse was posthumously awarded the Victoria Cross. Private John Cairns is commemorated on Special Memorial B18, and at the request of his widow (Elizabeth), the inscription reads *'Rest in Peace Amen'.*

While the graves at Obozerskaya Burial Ground were thought to be lost to time and the elements, in recent times (2018), some of those have been discovered and the remains identified. A team of Russian volunteers, following a ten-year search under the guidance of Alexey Suhanovsky, found several graves in a metal scrapyard in the Obozerskaya region, and it's almost certain that three of the remains were those of Sgt Pearse, Private John Stoddart and Private John Cairns all killed on 29th August 1919. This discovery came from a cross-referencing of a 1919 RAF map showing a portion of the cemetery and a hand-drawn map created by Harry Creed of the Imperial War Graves Commission when he visited North Russia in 1925, tasked with locating and documenting the graves of British soldiers from the Intervention period. Having calculated the cemetery's location, Alexey and his team began searching for the graves in December 2017 by probing the frozen ground beneath the metal scrapyard. After discovering some interesting leads, the team postponed the search until the following summer when a more detailed investigation could be conducted on the thawed area.

Then, in early June 2018, the team discovered what they believed to be the location of two graves, and it was decided to exhume one of the bodies to try and determine if it was the remains of a British soldier. The remains were believed to be that of a member of an RAF regiment as the woollen tunic found with the remains had buttons bearing the crest of the RAF.[88] Curiously, at the head of the coffin were perfectly preserved flowers shaped into a dandelion chain placed there almost one hundred years ago. This allowed Alexey to identify the remains, as the only RAF casualty buried in Obozerskaya cemetery when dandelions were in bloom was Joseph Damms, a 19-year-old Air Mechanic from Birmingham, England, buried in grave number 13, according to Creed's map. From this reference point, Alexey's team calculated the location of VC winner Samuel Pearse's resting place at grave number 16, just a few metres north of Damm's grave.

Digging commenced at this location, and just 130 centimetres below the surface, they discovered a coffin and remains which, following an autopsy, were eventually identified as that of Sgt Samuel Pearse VC MM. This positive identification means that the location of the remains of Private John Cairns, in grave number 15, can confidently be identified. Also buried in this cemetery are the remains of Cpl Peter Mulhall (see chapter 12) and Private Henry Begley (see chapter 13). Since the re-discovery of this cemetery, which holds the remains of 27 Allied soldiers, including VC winner Sgt Samuel Pearse, a campaign has begun to re-inter those remains in a more dignified setting (for more about this campaign, see https://www.samuelpearsevc.com.au/)

Aftermath

Following his death, John Cairns' widow, Elizabeth, met and fell in love with Robert George Cassidy. Cassidy had emigrated to the US in 1911; this was his first time back in Belfast in twenty years. The pair got married, and in 1934, Robert Cassidy brought his new bride (Elizabeth Cairns) back to New York with him. The pair returned to Belfast in 1936 to collect Elizabeth's 24-year-old daughter and bring her back to America.

Elizabeth Cassidy lived and worked in New York with her husband, Robert, until she died in 1959. Robert died in 1955, and both are buried in St Lawrence Martyr R.C. Cemetery in Suffolk County, New York.

Elizabeth Cairns, John's only daughter, married John Fiore in New York in 1938 and, according to the 1950 Brooklyn census, had four children: Carmela (11), Eliza (9), Joan Ann (8), and Patricia (5). Elizabeth Fiore died in August 1986 and is buried in the Holy Sepulchre cemetery in Suffolk County, New York.

Chapter 22

Pte John Mahoney 46th Royal Fusiliers (Cork)

John Mahoney was born in Cork in November 1888 to Denis and Mary (nee Colbert). He was the eldest and the only male of the three children born to the family. His father, John, worked in the local brewery, Beamish & Crawford, as a cooper and the family lived on the south side of Cork City in the Evergreen/Friar's Walk area. John's mother, Mary, following the birth of her third child, Elizabeth, in 1894, fell ill with Tuberculosis, which was rampant among the squalid conditions in the tenements in Cork city at the time. Mary eventually became so ill that she was moved to the Cork workhouse on the Douglas Road, which later became St Finbarr's Hospital.

John was only 6 years of age when his mother, Mary, died of TB in the workhouse. For his father, Denis, to continue working in the brewery, his aunt, Mary Mahoney (54), moved in with them and helped Denis raise his three children, John, Elizabeth and Hannah (Mary). When John left school at the age of 15, he followed his father into Beamish & Crawford as a cooper, but in 1907, at the age of 18, John decided that the army life was for him and enlisted in the 1st Battalion of the Royal Munster Fusiliers. When war broke out in August 1914, the Battalion was stationed in Rangoon, Burma and was ordered to return to Britain and await further orders. In March 1915, they embarked from Avonmouth for the Balkans. Their mission was to open the Dardanelles, the closing of which had brought the Ottoman Empire into the war on the side of the Germans. Now, the Allies believed that opening a second front in the east to defeat the Ottomans could also facilitate a route to their ally Russia and thus undermine and break the stalemate on the Western Front.

The 1ˢᵗ battalion of the Munster Fusiliers consisted of 28 officers and 1,002 other ranks, including Private John Mahoney from Cork. The plan called for an amphibious landing by French and British troops on the Gallipoli peninsula to march inland and secure the Dardanelles. The Munsters were tasked with landing at Cape Helles at the foot of the peninsula, advancing 10km and seizing the heights of Achi Baba. However, the beach landings didn't go as planned as hidden Turkish machine gun posts were awaiting the Munsters, and they were decimated as they attempted to land on the Cape Helles beaches. Caught between the sea and the machine guns on the high ground, the troops didn't stand a chance, and one eye-witness remarked that we '…were literally slaughtered like rats in a trap. Many men sank due to the weight of their equipment and were drowned…dead and wounded lay at the water's edge tinted crimson from their blood'.[89] Luckily, Mahoney survived the slaughter and went on to fight in Egypt in January 1916 and the Western Front in April of the same year, where he served with the 2ⁿᵈ Battalion of the Munsters. John Mahoney was in Lille when the Armistice was signed on 11ᵗʰ November 1918. He returned to England and was awaiting demobilisation when the call went out for 'volunteers' to serve in one last campaign in North Russia.

Mahoney duly enlisted in the 46ᵗʰ Battalion of the Royal Fusiliers and embarked in late May on board HMS *Praetorian* for Murmansk. After spending three days in Murmansk, the troops sailed for Archangel, arriving on June 6, 1919. After a week in Archangel, Mahoney's battalion embarked on a barge on the River Dvina bound for Osinova, about 200 miles away. Mahoney spent the next two months attempting to push the Bolsheviks back and was also involved in the August 10ᵗʰ offensive that resulted in heavy casualties for the Russians.

Despite these heavy losses, the Bolsheviks were emboldened by the Allies' decision to withdraw from North Russia. The withdrawal plan also had a demoralising effect on many of the White Russian forces, who now began to mutiny and go over to the Bolshevik side. On 11ᵗʰ September, the Bolsheviks launched an attack on Troitsa, where Mahoney was billeted, and in the ensuing battle, John Mahoney was killed. Many of the Bolshevik attackers were later identified as deserters from the North Russian Rifles who had mutinied and murdered their officers in July 1919.

Memorial service to the fallen in Troitsa (UBC Library D559. A14 1919)

Private John Mahoney was buried in the field, and a memorial was erected in Troitsa to the British troops who were killed in the vicinity. Following the evacuation of North Russia, this memorial was destroyed by the Bolsheviks. He is now commemorated on 'stone no.5' in the Archangel cemetery in the Russian Federation.

The last Irish casualty in the North Russian campaign was Private John Mahoney, and within two weeks of his death, all British troops had been successfully withdrawn from Archangel. Mahoney's father and sisters were heartbroken when they received the news of John's death so far from home. A family notice was placed in the local newspaper (Evening Echo) on each anniversary of his death up to 1933.

IN MEMORIAM.

O'MAHONY—Fourteenth Anniversary—In loving memory of Private John O'Mahony, Royal Fusiliers, late 41 Douglas Street, killed in North Russia on 12th September, 1919. Jesus. have mercy on his soul.— (Inserted by his fond father and sisters).

Evening Echo 12 September 1933 p.8

John Mahoney's father died in 1946 in Cork.

Conclusion

The final evacuation of North Russia took place in late September 1919. By the 23rd, the entire force had withdrawn to the inner defence line around Archangel. Then, on September 27th, the final soldier left the quay of Archangel, and General Yevgeny (Eugene) Miller, the chief of the North Russian armed forces, declared a curfew. Ironside provides an emotional description of his last hours in Archangel on board the yacht of Admiral Sir John Green as they prepared to sail from Archangel's pier.

> ...*the signalman on the bridge reported that two officers were emerging from among the buildings of the port and heading for the pier. They were General Miller and his ADC, Count Hamilton, a lieutenant in the Russian Navy. They looked strangely forlorn as they walked slowly down the long stretch of the pier. They were the only human beings in sight.*[90]

Both Russians came on board to bid Ironside farewell; following the inspection of the guard, Ironside thanked Millar for his help in making the British withdrawal safe and peaceful. Millar was then piped off the yacht.

> *We stood watching them as they walked slowly away. I was half hoping that he might turn and wave his hand to us in farewell, but he never looked back, keeping steadily on till they disappeared behind the buildings once more. He was a very proud and gallant gentleman.*[91]

A convoy of 45 ships sailed out of Archangel bound for England via Murmansk, and General Miller was now left alone with his dwindling army to face the might of the Red Army. By February 1920, the Whites were on the verge of defeat and started negotiations with the Bolsheviks regarding surrender terms, but the only terms offered were 'unconditional surrender'.[92] On the 19th of February, Millar, together with several White

Russian officers, fled on board icebreaker *Kazma Minin* for Murmansk. Shortly after, the 154th Red Infantry Regiment marched unopposed into Archangel and two days later took Murmansk. Millar eventually settled in Paris, where in 1937, he was lured to an apartment, drugged, and smuggled back to Russia, where he was executed on 11th May 1939.[93]

Thus ended the ill-fated military intervention by the Allies in North Russia, which helped to bolster the Bolsheviks' standing and position in Russia and their Red Army as a superior fighting machine. Politically, the intervention created a rift in the East/ West divide that still exists more than one hundred years later.[94] While most of the US troops killed in North Russia were repatriated home, nearly all the allied troops, including 19 of the 21 Irish-born casualties, still lie in the graves where they were laid to rest in Russia.

Appendix 1

One other Irish casualty was identified who died in Russia during the period in question (1918 – 1919), but because it was considered outside the scope (North Russia) of this research, it was not included in the main body of the work. The following provides a brief overview of the untimely death of 25-year-old Corkman Denis O'Connell.

Stoker Denis O'Connell Royal Navy (Cork)

Born in 1893, Denis O'Connell was the fourth child of Denis and Mary, who lived in Curraghconway on the slopes of the hills overlooking the south side of Cork City. His father, Denis, was a coachman and domestic servant who worked for some of the wealthier families around that area. The family would have two more children, Mary, born in 1896, and John, born in 1898. As was usual for working-class families then, the children left school early, and Denis found work as a general labourer in Cork City. His brother Michael got a job with the railway as a porter, and his younger brother Daniel followed in his father's footsteps and worked as a servant in one of the big houses owned by the Hodders in Ballea, Co Cork.

When Denis was almost 17, he decided to enlist in the Royal Navy and duly presented himself to the local naval base in Queenstown (Cobh) to make an application. At the time (1910), the Royal Navy was on a recruiting campaign, as with the introduction of the more efficient 'water-tube boiler', a replacement for the cylindrical boiler, many more 'stokers' were needed to tend to these boilers.

Because of this vast shortage of 'stokers, ' the recruitment process was not as strict as it should be, and one commentator has claimed that 'It is clear from the evidence presented that individual recruitment officers cut corners and entered men who fell short of the official physical entry requirements for stokers'.[95] However, because stokers needed to be

18 years of age, O'Connell lied about his age and gave his date of birth as 2nd December 1890 (making him 20 years of age) instead of his actual date of birth, which meant he was just 16 years and 11 months. At the time, recruits were not obliged to produce their birth certificates, and because Denis must have looked older than his age, he was enlisted as a Royal Navy stoker on 11th November 1910 for 12 years' service. The pay for a Stoker 2nd class who signed up for 12 years was 1/8 per day or nearly 12 shillings per week with free board and lodging, rising to 2/1 per day on promotion to Stoker 1st class; this must have seemed like a good deal for O'Connell compared to life as a general labourer in Cork.

He was sent to the Royal Navy barracks at Devenport to be trained at the Stokers and Engine Room Artificers School named HMS *Vivid II*. The work of a stoker was hard and dangerous. Chamberlain claims that:

> ...stokers had arguably the most physically demanding and dangerous occupation than any man onboard. They worked in claustrophobic coal-bunkers devoid of breathable air or in front of roaring furnaces deep in the bowels of the ship where escape in time of emergency was almost impossible.[96]

With the advent of the Great War, things only got more complicated and perilous. Nevertheless, O'Connell seemed happy at his job as within a year of enlisting, he was promoted to Stoker 1st Class and by May 1917 was Leading Stoker, which meant he had participated in a prescribed Mechanical Training course and successfully passed the examination at the end of the course. He was also trained in working on submarines, and life as a submariner stoker meant a considerable improvement in living and working conditions that had been his lot on the various ships he served on throughout the war.

At the war's end, Leading Stoker Denis O'Connell was assigned to HMS *Lucia*, which was once the German ship *Spreewald*, captured in 1914 and converted to a submarine depot ship. O'Connell was attached to HMS *L55*, an L-class British submarine laid down in 1917 and commissioned on 9th December 1918. HMS *Lucia* and her flotilla of submarines were stationed at Teesside, but early in 1919, they were ordered to support the British campaign in the Baltics, codenamed *Operation Red Trek*. This campaign aimed to suppress the Bolsheviks' ability to expand into the Baltics, protect British interests, and support the independence of the newly established countries of Estonia and Latvia. HMS *Lucia* left Teesside on 13th May 1919 with a flotilla of 5 submarines, including L55, to which Leading Stoker Denis O'Connell was attached. The Baltic fleet, including the submarines, were taking part in defensive and offensive manoeuvres – defending the independence of the newly formed states and attacking the Bolshevik vessels based at Kronstadt, attempting to break the British blockade.

Less than a month after arriving in the Baltics, O'Connell's L55 attacked two Russian destroyers, Gavriil and Azard, laying mines around the Koporye Bay in the Russian part of the Gulf of Finland. After firing torpedoes that missed their target, L55 was, in turn, attacked by both destroyers and, attempting to make a quick getaway, strayed into one of their own minefields and was sunk. While the Bolsheviks claimed one of their destroyers hit the submarine, it is more likely that a mine destroyed the submarine with the loss of all lives, including Denis O'Connell, on board.

His mother, Mary, now a widow, received the news of Denis' death at her home on the Pouladuff road in Cork. At the time, three of her sons were serving in the Royal Navy – William (29), Daniel (26), and Denis, whose age was given as 28 on the Royal Navy obituary but, in reality, was just 25.

Aftermath

In 1927, the Russians managed to locate and salvage L55. It became part of the Soviet fleet as a training vessel and was used as a design template for the Soviet L-class submarines that followed.

Following protracted negotiations with the British, the Soviet government allowed the bodies of those recovered to be repatriated to Britain but would only allow a merchant ship, and not a warship, to collect the remains. The British sent merchant ship *Truro* to collect the remains of 34 of the 42 crew that were lost and, after leaving Soviet waters, transferred the remains to HMS *Champion*, who returned the bodies to Britain.

HMS *Champion* **with the remains of the crew of L55**

The bodies were reinterred in a communal grave in Haslar Royal Navy cemetery in Gosport, Portsmouth, on 7th September 1928. It's unclear if any of Denis O'Connell's family members attended the funeral, but they would have been invited.

In 2015, when Estonia was preparing to celebrate its 100th anniversary, it was decided to invite family members of those who were killed protecting Estonia's independence between 1918 and 1920. In an attempt to contact Denis O'Connell's family, a letter was sent to the Irish Examiner, but no relative came forward.

Was lead submarine stoker Denis O'Connell a relative of yours?

On June 4, 1919, HM Submarine L55 sank in the Baltic Sea. L55 had been targeting two Bolshevik warships. It is unclear whether the submarine was sunk by Bolshevik gunfire or from straying into a British-laid minefield.

The presence of the British navy in the Baltic Sea area contributed to the Baltic states of Estonia, Latvia and Lithuania achieving independence after the First World War.

Denis O'Connell was a leading stoker on the (11), Michael (10), David (8), Denis (7), Mary (5), John (3). The O'Connell family in 1911 was, as follows: Denis (49) coachman, domestic servant; Mary (50) from Co. Waterford; Michael (20) railway porter; Denis (18) general labourer; Mary Margaret (16); John (13).

Estonians are preparing to celebrate 100 years of independence and it would be a fitting tribute to the part played by Denis O'Connell if a representative of the O'Connell family could attend.

Irish Examiner 11/05/2015 p.10

Bibliography

Barry, J.M. (2004) *The Great Influenza: The Story of the Deadliest Plague in History,* New York: Viking Press.

Barry, T. (1981) *Guerilla Days in Ireland,* Dublin: Anvil Books.

Bianchi, A. P. (2023) "Has the U.S. ever fought on Russian soil? You'd be surprised" in *National Geographic,* 8th August, 2023.

Blumberg, H.E. (1927) *Britain's Sea Soldiers: A record of the Royal Marines during the war* 1914 – 1919, Devonport: Swiss & Co., Naval and Military printers and publishers.

Broadberry, S.N. (1990) "Macroeconomic Trends in Britain during the Trans-World War I Period" in *The Economic History Review,* 43 (2), 271-282.

Buchan, J. (1920) *The Long Road to Victory,* London: Thomas Nelson & Son.

Bujack, J. (2008) *Undefeated: The Extraordinary Life and Death of Lt. Col. Jack Sherwood-Kelly* VC, DSO, CMG, Haywards Heath: Foster Consulting.

Burnell, T. (2016) 'County by county in the South, a roll call of the dead was slowly compiled', *Irish Times* 01/07/2016 pg.10.

Chamberlain, T. (2013) Stokers – *The Lowest of the Low? A Social History of Royal Navy Stokers* 1850 – 1950, University of Exeter (Unpublished Thesis).

Churchill Project (2020) Hillsdale College, available at https:// winstonchurchill.hillsdale.edu/articles/ Accessed 31/08/2020.

Collins, S. (2014) 'Records of 49,000 Irish WW1 dead in new digital archive', *Irish Times* 10/01/2014

Cullen, S., (2019) *The Impact of the Irish Revolution on a Garrison County: Kildare 1912-1923*, Dublin City University (Unpublished Thesis).

Falls, C., (1940) *Military Operations. France and Belgium, 1917: The German Retreat to the Hindenburg Line and the Battle of Arras*, London: Macmillan.

Foley, P. (1999) "The Carlow Workhouse" in *Carloviana* (47) pp.7-14 available at https://carlowhistorical.com/wp-content/uploads/2016/01/ Carloviana-No-47-1999. Accessed 25/06/2022

Halliday, E.M., (1961) T*he Ignorant Armies, The Anglo-American Archangel Expedition 1918 -1919*, London: Weidenfeld & Nelson.

Imperial War Museum, (2024) 'Why men of Ireland volunteered to fight in the First World War', available at https://www.iwm.org.uk/history/ why-men-of-ireland-volunteered-to-fight-in-the-first-world-warIreland. Accessed 14/06/2024.

Ironside, E. (1953) *Archangel 1918 –19*, London: Constable.

Irwin, M. (2003) *Victoria's Cross: The story of Sgt. Samuel George Pearse VC MM from Anzac to Archangel*, Northland Centre Victoria: Mike Irwin.

Johnson, J.H. (1990) "The Context of Migration: The example of Ireland in the 19 th century", in *Transactions of the Institute of British Geographers*, Vol.15 (3) pp.259-276.

Kehoe, S.K. (2004) *Special Daughters of Rome: Glasgow and its Roman Catholic Sisters 1847 – 1913*, University of Glasgow (Unpublished Thesis).

Kendall, P. (2016) *The Zeebrugge Raid 1918: A story of courage and sacrifice*, Barnsley: Frontline Books.

Kinvig, C. (2006) *Churchill's Crusade: The British Invasion of Russia 1918-1920*, London: Hambleton Continuum.

Luddy, M. (2011) "Unmarried Mothers in Ireland 1880 – 1973" in *Women's History Review*, Vol. 20, No. 1, 109-126.

Marriot-Dodington, W., (1919) *Extracts from the Regimental Chronicles of the Oxfordshire & Buckinghamshire Light Infantry*, available at http://www.lightbobs.com/1919.html accessed 9/4/2021.

McGreevy, R. (2018) 'Historian lists almost 30,000 Irishmen who died in WW1', *Irish Times* 11/11/2018.

McGreevy, R. (2018) "John Redmond and the First World War in *Studies: An Irish Quarterly Review,* Vol.107 (428), pp.407-418.

McLeod, J. (2015) *Gallipoli,* Oxford: OUP.

Mougel, N. (2011) 'World War 1 Casualties' in *Reperes,* CVCE available at https://www.studocu.com/es/document/universidad-de-navarra/law-and-the-state/s-world-war-i-casualties-en/47011127 accessed 31/08/2022.

Provincial Archives of Alberta: *Homestead Records,* available at https://www.provincialarchives.alberta.ca/sites/default/files/2020-09/HomesteadRecords.pdf accessed 10/2/2023

Pyves, R.R. (2022) *Sir John James Taylor: de Facto Ruler of Ireland,* Published by Amazon.

Ray, M. (2024) 'Selective Service Acts: United States Laws' in *Encyclopaedia Britannica.* Available at: https://www.britannica.com/topic/Selective-Service-Act Accessed January 2025.

'Remains of long-lost Australian Digger Sam Pearse', *ABC 7.30 (2019),* available at https://www.abc.net.au/7.30/remains-of-long-lost-australian-digger-sam-pearse/11544588 Accessed 13 June 2022.

Ryan, C. B. (1916-1919) 'Diary' available at https://quod.lib.umich.edu/p/polar/86620.0001.001/1?rgn=full+text;view=image accessed 12 July 2024.

Shapiro, S. (1973) 'Intervention in Russia (1918 – 1919)', *United States Institute Proceedings,* vol. 99/4/842, April 1973, pp.52-61

Shrive, F.J. (1981) *The Diary of a P.B.O. (Poor Bloody Observer),* Ontario: Boston Mills Press.

Singleton-Gates, G.R. (1920) *Bolos and Barishynas: Being an account of the doings of the Sadlier-Jackson Brigade, and Altham Flotilla, on the North Dvina during the summer 1919,* Aldershot: Gale & Polden.

Steel, N., & Hart, P. (1994) *Defeat at Gallipoli,* London: Macmillan.

Steuer, K. (2008) *Pursuit of an "Unparalleled Opportunity": The American YMCA and Prisoner-of-War Diplomacy among the Central Power Nations During World War 1, 1914-1923,* Columbia: Columbia University Press.

Strachan, H. (2004) *The First World War,* Vol.1 Oxford: OUP.

Strakhovsky, L.I. (1958) "The Canadian Artillery Brigade in North Russia, 1918 – 1919" in the *Canadian Historical Review,* Vol. XXXIX (2) pp.125-146.

Vermeiren, J. (2018) 'The Tannenberg myth in literature and history 1914-1945', *European Review of History,* vol. 25 (5), pp.778-802.

Walsh, J.E. (2001-2002) 'The Strange Sad Death of Sergeant Kenney: A Personal Story of Heroism and Loss during America's Russian Intervention', in The *Wisconsin Magazine of History,* Vol. 85 (2), pp. 2-17.

Wright, D. (2017) *Churchill's Secret War with Lenin: British and Commonwealth Military Intervention in the Russian Civil War 1918 -1920*, Solihull: Helion and Company.

Wright, D. (2024) *Australia's Lost Heros: Anzacs in the Russian Civil War 1919*, Newport NSW: Big Sky Publishing.

Wyrall, E. (1999[1932]) *The 19th Division* 1914-1918, Uckfield: Naval & Military Press.

Archival Documents

WO 95/5430 War diaries, 2nd (Sadlier Jackson) Brigade, 45th & 46th Battalions.

WO 95/3144/2 War Diary 5th Battalion Connaught Rangers.

WO 339/12950 Military Service File Major Francis Mortimer D. Taylor RAMC.

1901 and 1911 census of Ireland available at https://www.census. nationalarchives.ie accessed January 2024.

Gazette Dispatches

London Gazette 23 July 1918, Zeebrugge Raid, (Capt. Edward Bamford).

London Gazette 14 May 1919, Kodish Operations North Russia, (Capt. (Acting Major), Frank Mortimer Taylor).

Supplement to the Edinburgh Gazette 1 August 1919, North Russia, (Lt. William Frederick Bassett).

Index

W

Waterford 28, 33,123, 124, 134

Western Front 1, 2,4, 5, 10, 11, 24, 25, 28, 29, 36, 37, 44, 66, 75, 76, 78, 79, 80, 85, 86, 91, 92, 98,108, 109, 110, 111, 114,123, 131, 136, 147, 148

Y

Ypres 75, 76, 78, 79,80, 84, 108, 111, 142

Z

Zeebrugge 17, 21, 22, 159, 162, 172

Endnotes

Introduction

1 Jan Vermeiren, 'The Tannenberg myth in literature and history 1914-1945', European Review of History, vol. 25, No. 5, 2018, pp.778-802.

2 Hew Strachan, The First World War, Vol.1 (Oxford: OUP 2004), pp.300-310.

3 Imperial War Museum, (2024) 'Why men of Ireland volunteered to fight in the First World War', available at https://www.iwm.org.uk/history/why-men-of-ireland-volunteered-to-fight-in-the-first-worldwar#. accessed 14/06/2024

4 Tom Barry, (1981) Guerilla Days in Ireland, (Dublin: Anvil Books) p.2

5 Nadege Mougel, (2011) 'World War 1 Casualties' in Reperes, CVCE available at http://www.centre-robert-schuman.org/userfiles/files/REPERES. accessed 31/08/2022

6 Ronan McGreevy, (2018) 'Historian lists almost 30,000 Irishmen who died in WW1', Irish Times 11/11/2018

7 Stephen Collins, (2014) 'Records of 49,000 Irish WW1 dead in new digital archive', Irish Times 10/01/2014

8 Tom Burnell, (2016) 'County by county in the South, a roll call of the dead was slowly compiled', Irish Times 01/07/2016.

9 Damien Wright, (2017) Churchill's Secret War with Lenin: British and Commonwealth Military Intervention in the Russian Civil War 1918 -1920, (Solihull: Helion and Company 2017), p.29.

10 Clifford Kinvig, Churchill's Crusade: The British Invasion of

Russia 1918-1920, (London: Hambleton Continuum, 2006) p.164.

11 Churchill Project, Bolshevism…Foul baboonery…Strangle at Birth, Hillsdale College, March 2016.

12 Wright, Churchill's Secret War, p.30.

Chapter 1

13 Ernest M Halliday, The Ignorant Armies, The Anglo-American Archangel Expedition 1918 - 1919 (London : Weidenfeld & Nelson 1961), pp.17-18.

Chapter 2

14 Halliday, The Ignorant Armies, p.64

15 Charles Brady Ryan, (1916-1919) 'Diary', available at https://quod.lib.umich.edu/ accessed 12 July 2024.

16 Halliday, The Ignorant Armies, pp.82/3

17 For more on the Polar Bear Memorial see Mike Grobbel's excellent and informative "Detroit's Own" Polar Bear Association @ "Detroit's Own" Polar Bear Memorial Association (grobbel.org) accessed 12/6/2024.

Chapter 4

18 James H. Johnson, "The Context of Migration: The example of Ireland in the 19th century", Transactions of the Institute of British Geographers, Vol.15, No.3, 1990, pp.259-276.

19 Sara K. Kehoe, Special Daughters of Rome: Glasgow and its Roman Catholic Sisters 1847 – 1913, University of Glasgow, (Unpublished Thesis 2004).

20 Paul Kendall, (2016) The Zeebrugge Raid 1918: A story of courage and sacrifice, Barnsley: Frontline Books, p.346.

21 No. 30807 The London Gazette (Supplement), 23 July 1918, p. 8586.

22 Ibid.

23 Herbert E. Blumberg, (1927) Britain's Sea Soldiers: A record of the Royal Marines during the war 1914 – 1919, Devonport: Swiss & Co., Naval and Military printers and publishers.

24 John M. Barry, (2004) The Great Influenza: The Story of the Deadliest Plague in History, New York: Viking Press.

25 Ibid.

26 Wright, Churchill's Secret War, p.123.

27 Leonid Strakhovsky 1944 in Wright, Churchill's Secret War, p.124.

Chapter 5

28 2608 Supplement To The Edinburgh Gazette, August 1, 1919. Lt. William Frederick Bassett, 10th Bn.R. Highrs., attd. 2/10th Bn. R. Scots (N. Russia).

29 John Buchan, (1920) The Long Road to Victory, Thomas Nelson & Son: London p.315

Chapter 6

30 When members of the Cunney family emigrated to America, they changed their name to Kenney for simplification purposes. This chapter will follow that format, naming them as Cunney while in Ireland and changing their name to Kenney following their arrival in America.

31 Michael Ray (2024) 'Selective Service Acts: United States Laws' in Encyclopaedia Britannica. Available at: https://www.britannica. com/topic/Selective-Service-Act (accessed January 2025).

32 John Evangelist Walsh, (2001-2002) 'The Strange Sad Death of Sergeant Kenney: A Personal Story of Heroism and Loss during America's Russian Intervention', in The Wisconsin Magazine of History, Vol. 85 (2), p7.

33 Halliday, The Ignorant Armies, p.107

34 Walsh, The Strange Sad Death of Sergeant Kenney, pp.7/8

35 Ibid.

36 Charles Brady-Ryan, Diary

37 Halliday, The Ignorant Armies, p.104.

38 Ibid.

39 Walsh, The Strange Sad Death of Sergeant Kenney, p14.

40 Halliday, The Ignorant Armies, p.196.

Chapter 7

41 Provincial Archives of Alberta available at https://www.provincialarchives.alberta.ca/sites/default/files/2020-09/Homestead%20Records.pdf accessed 10/2/2023

42 Strakhovsky, Leonid, (1958) "The Canadian Artillery Brigade in North Russia, 1918 – 1919", Canadian Historical Review, 1958, Vol. XXXIX (2) pp.128/9

43 Frank J. Shrive, (1981) The Diary of a P.B.O. (Poor Bloody Observer), Ontario: Boston Mills Press p.64

44 Shrive, The Diary of a P.B.O, p.80

45 Wright, Churchill's Secret War, p.164.

46 Edmond Ironside, (1953) Archangel 1918 –19, London: Constable, p.106

Chapter 8

47 Military Service File of Major Francis Mortimer D. Taylor, RAMC WO/339/12950.

48 London Gazette May 14th 1919.

49 Halliday, The Ignorant Armies, p.104

50 Military Service File of Major Francis Mortimer D. Taylor, RAMC WO/339/12950.

51 Ibid.

52 Richard R. Pyves, (2022) Sir John James Taylor: de Facto Ruler of Ireland, Published by Amazon, p.80/1.

53 Ibid.

54 Irish Times 8th August 1919, p.4.

55 Stephen N. Broadberry, "Macroeconomic Trends in Britain during the Trans-World War I Period" in The Economic History Review, Vol. 43, No. 2, May 1990, p.271.

Chapter 9

56 Wilfrid Marriot-Dodington, (1919) Extracts from the Regimental Chronicles of the Oxfordshire & Buckinghamshire Light Infantry, available at http://www.lightbobs.com/1919.html accessed 12/6/2023.

57 Wright, Churchill's Secret War, pp.202/3.

58 Marriot-Dodington, Extracts from the Regimental Chronicles, p.2

Chapter 10

59 Wright, Churchill's Secret War, p.203

60 All correspondence with Margaret O'Driscoll is available at the Commonwealth War Graves Commission under CWGC/8/1/4/1/1/203 (AA59925) 1934/1935.

Chapter 11

61 Wright, Churchill's Secret War, p.60.

62 Ibid

Chapter 12

63 WO 95/5430 War diaries, 2nd Brigade.

Chapter 13

64 WO 95/3144/2 War Diary of 5th Battalion Connaught Rangers.

65 WO 95/5422, War Diaries, 1st (Grogan's) Brigade.

66 Jack Bujack, (2008) Undefeated: The Extraordinary Life and Death of Lt. Col. Jack Sherwood-Kelly VC,DSO,CMG, (Haywards Heath: Foster Consulting), p 205.

Interlude

67 Wright, Churchill's Secret War, p.223.

68 Wright, Churchill's Secret War, p.254.

Chapter 15

69 Ronan McGreevy, (2018) "John Redmond and the First World War in Studies: An Irish Quarterly Review, Vol.107 (428) p.409.

70 Everard Wyrall, (1999 [1932]) The 19th Division 1914-1918, Uckfield: The Naval and Military Press, pp.44-48.

71 Wyrall, The 19th Division, p.68.

72 Wyrall, The 19thDivision, 1999: 66.

73 Wyrall, The 19th Division, 1999.

74 G.R.Singleton-Gates, Bolos and Barishynas: Being an account of the doings of the Sadlier-Jackson Brigade, and Altham Flotilla, on the North Dvina during the summer 1919 (Aldershot: Gale & Polden, 1920) pp.13/14.

75 Singleton-Gates, Bolos and Barishynas, p.95.

76 Wright, Churchill's Secret War, p.95.

77 Wright, Churchill's Secret War, p.278

78 Ibid. p243

79 For more on Sgt Pearse see Damien Wright, (2024) Australia's Lost Heros: Anzacs in the Russian Civil War 1919, Newport NSW: Big Sky Publishing.

Chapter 17

80 Kenneth, Steuer, Pursuit of an "Unparalleled Opportunity":
    The American YMCA and Prisoner-of-War Diplomacy among
    the Central Power Nations During World War 1, 1914-1923
    (Columbia: CUP, 2008) p.2.

81 Singleton-Gates, Bolos and Barishynas, p.106

Chapter 18

82 Maria Luddy, "Unmarried Mothers in Ireland 1880 – 1973",
    Women's History Review, Vol. 20, No. 1, January 2011, p.111.

83 Jenny McLeod, (2015) Gallipoli (Oxford: OUP, 2015), p.38

84 Patrick Foley, "The Carlow Workhouse", Carloviana: Journal of
    the old Carlow society, (47) December 1999. p.7.

Chapter 20

85 Cyril Falls, Military Operations. France and Belgium, 1917: The
    German Retreat to the Hindenburg Line and the Battle of Arras
    (London: Macmillan, 1940) pp.243-247.

86 Irish Census 1911, available at https://www.census.
    nationalarchives.ie accessed January 2024.

Chapter 21

87 Mike Irwin, Victoria's Cross: The story of Sgt. Samuel George
    Pearse, V.C. M.M.: from Anzac to Archangel, (M.Irwin 2003), p.63

88 Wright, Damien. Australia's Lost Heroes: Anzacs in the Russian
    Civil War, Newport: 2024: 318

Chapter 22

89 Nigel Steel & Peter Hart, Defeat at Gallipoli, (London:
    Macmillan 1994) pp.90-91.

Conclusion

90 Edmund Ironside, Archangel 1918-1919, (London: Constable,
    1953) p.186.

91   Ibid.

92   Halliday, The Ignorant Armies, p.209.

93   Wright, Churchill's Secret War, p.295.

94   Andrea P. Bianchi, 'Have the U.S. ever fought on Russian Soil? You'd be surprised', National Geographic, 8th August 2023.

Appendix

95   Tony Chamberlain, Stokers – The Lowest of the Low? A Social History of Royal Navy Stokers 1850 – 1950, University of Exeter (Unpublished Thesis 2013) p.312.

96   Chamberlain, Stokers, p.263

HIGH FIVE TO THE BOYS

a CELEBRATION of ACE AUSTRALIAN MEN

RANDOM HOUSE AUSTRALIA

A Random House book
Published by Penguin Random House Australia Pty Ltd
Level 3, 100 Pacific Highway, North Sydney NSW 2060
penguin.com.au

Penguin
Random House
Australia

First published by Random House Australia in 2018

A catalogue record for this
book is available from the
National Library of Australia

NATIONAL
LIBRARY
OF AUSTRALIA

ISBN 978 0 14379 178 2

Cover and internal design by Astred Hicks, Design Cherry
Printed in China

Penguin Random House Australia uses papers that are natural, renewable and
recyclable products and made from wood grown in sustainable forests. The logging
and manufacturing processes are expected to conform to the environmental
regulations of the country of origin.

Every effort has been made to ensure that the facts presented in this book are correct.
Please contact the publisher regarding any errors to ensure they are rectified in
subsequent editions. Please also note that the biographies of the featured men are not
encyclopedic accounts of their lives and accomplishments.

Aboriginal and Torres Strait Islander readers are advised that this book contains
images and names of deceased persons.

HIGH FIVE

noun, colloquial
a public salutation to
express gratitude or solidarity

CONTENTS

Inside this book you will find men from Australia's past and present — but they're all taking us towards a better future. You'll find Australian men young and old, loud and quiet, funny and serious, artistic and sporty, curious and determined.

Above all, you will find men to be proud of!

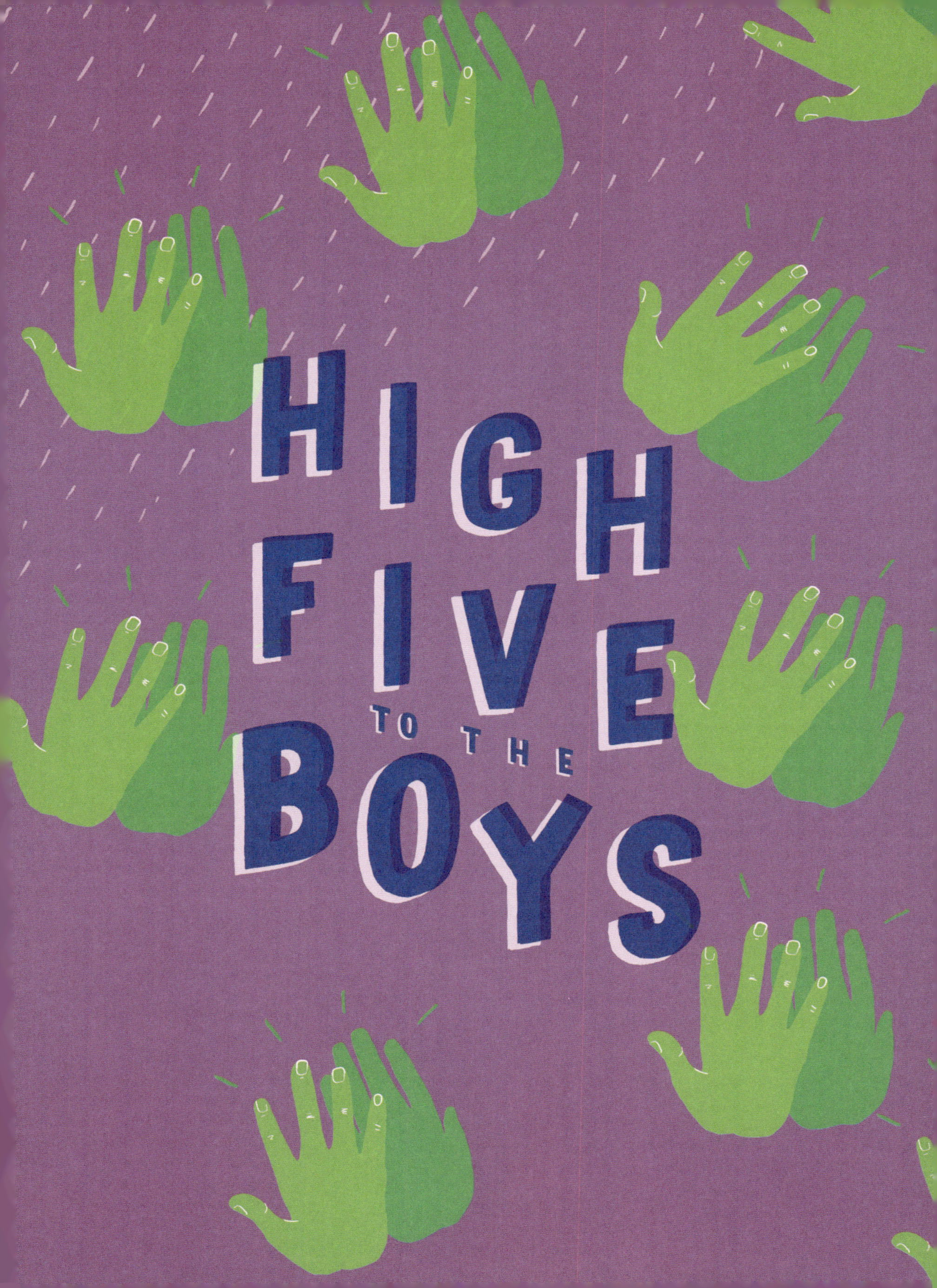
HIGH FIVE
TO THE
BOYS

A HIGH FIVE TO

ADAM GOODES

FOR PLAYING FAIR ON AND OFF THE FIELD

Cheer, cheer
the sportsmen
who play with
determination
and courage,
and use their
success on the
field to create
opportunities for
others.

ADAM GOODES

(1980–)

The name Adam Goodes is synonymous with the red and white of the Sydney Swans – the talented footballer played seventeen seasons with the club. An Adnyamathanha and Narungga man, Adam spent his early years in South Australia and played soccer, but after moving to country Victoria he took up Aussie Rules and began to show huge potential in the game. He was scouted by the Swans at age 16, and during his career Adam was a two-time Premiership winner, a two-time Brownlow Medal winner and a member of the Indigenous Team of the Century.

A jack-of-all-trades on the field, off the field Adam is an anti-racism campaigner and a passionate advocate of the importance of education for young people. It is this charity and community work that led to Adam being named Australian of the Year in 2014 – the first footballer to have won the award.

Adam's charitable work has focused on the GO Foundation, which he established with fellow Swans player Michael O'Loughlin in 2009. The charity provides scholarships to Indigenous kids to help them further their education, dream big and achieve their goals.

Adam hung up his boots in 2015 but the accolades have continued. In 2017 he was made an honorary Doctor of Health Sciences by the University of Sydney for his contribution to Australian society.

Adam, you're an all-round legend! You lifted that noble banner high for the Swans and have since lifted up so many kids towards a brighter future.

We admire your GO.

ILLUSTRATION BY CHRIS NIXON

A HIGH FIVE TO

AKIRA ISOGAWA

FOR HIS
DESIGN FLAIR

A pat on
the back to
the craftsmen
who believe in
themselves
and work
hard to make
their dreams
come true.

AKIRA ISOGAWA

(1964-)

Born in Kyoto, Japan, Akira Isogawa immigrated to Australia when he was 21 years old. He studied fashion design at the Sydney Institute of Technology (now the Fashion Design Studio TAFE), where he created incredible, lavish costumes inspired by contemporary Japanese design.

When he graduated in 1993, Akira didn't want to work for a large fashion company. Instead, he opened his own boutique and launched his women's fashion label, *Akira*. It wasn't all smooth sailing. He worked around the clock, going door to door to sell his collections in department stores locally and abroad, and making financial sacrifices. But his work's unique colours and shapes quickly garnered a huge following, and his exquisite fabrics – often intricately dyed, printed, embroidered or even handpainted – became widely celebrated.

In 1996 Akira showed his collections at Mercedes Australian Fashion Week, and in 1998 he was one of the first Australians ever to show his collection in Paris. He's been named Designer of the Year at the Australian Fashion Industry Awards and been the subject of an exhibition at the National Gallery of Victoria.

Akira's designs are sought after worldwide. At home, he has designed costumes for the Sydney Dance Company and the Australian Ballet, and he's even featured on an Australian commemorative stamp for his contribution to the history of Australian fashion.

Akira, with your flair and determination, you continue to make your mark on Australian fashion.

We love your style!

ILLUSTRATION BY JEREMY LORD

A HIGH FIVE TO

ANDY GRIFFITHS

FOR INSPIRING A WHOLE GENERATION OF READERS

Let's hear it for the champions of literacy who bring the ridiculous and the sublime to stories that children can't get enough of.

ANDY GRIFFITHS

(1961–)

Andy Griffiths was born in Melbourne. As a child, he would constantly pester his mother with questions. When he grew up and became a high school teacher, students did it back to him. It was while teaching that he became determined to coax his class of reluctant readers into using words and their imaginations. He found a lot of his students thought books were boring, so he started writing funny stories for them to prove that reading wasn't dull at all.

He kept practising his writing and began to make photocopied collections of his stories to sell at markets. Andy's first book, *Just Tricking!*, was published in 1997 and another seven *Just!* books followed. followed. In 2011 he teamed again with his long-time illustrating partner Terry Denton to create *The 13-Storey Treehouse*. They're up to *The 91-Storey Treehouse* and still climbing.

When he was younger, Andy played in rock bands and dreamt of being like his heroes Alice Cooper or David Bowie. Now his seriously funny books have made him a hero to a whole generation of children. He's written more than 30 books and won dozens of children's choice awards.

Andy is also an ambassador for the Indigenous Literacy Foundation and works tirelessly for the ILF. He believes books should make children – and their parents – laugh and that all children should get a chance to love reading.

Andy, your books have made millions of us laugh and there is no sign of your talent or dedication slowing down.

We want to be as creative as you!

ILLUSTRATION BY DANIEL GRAY-BARNETT

A HIGH FIVE TO

ANDY THOMAS

FOR FLYING HIGH

Let's salute the quiet achievers who chase their dreams all the way over oceans and into space.

ANDY THOMAS

(1951–)

Born and raised in South Australia, Andy Thomas was curious about space from a young age. He would build all sorts of model rockets from plastic and cardboard and loved to read about science. By 27 he'd completed his studies, achieving a PhD in Mechanical Engineering from the University of Adelaide – Doctor Andrew Thomas, anyone?

Andy headed to the United States of America to work for an aeronautical company, where he researched 'dynamic instabilities' – otherwise known as 'making things fly better'. Although he was at the top of his field and knew just about all there is to know about the physics of flight, Andy still didn't think he had much chance of ever being an astronaut.

It was only after he turned 41 – 15 years after leaving Australia – that he was selected by the US National Aeronautics and Space Administration (NASA) to become an astronaut. It was another four years before he went on his first space flight.

Andy wasn't going to let a late start slow things down. He was the first Australian-born astronaut to go into space, and by the time he retired, 22 years later, Andy had spent nearly 200 days in zero gravity, seen 16 sunsets in a day, and watched meteors pass below him.

Andy, you've shown us all that studying hard and working harder can help us achieve things that might seem far beyond our reach – no matter where we start.

We want to aim for the stars like you.

ILLUSTRATION BY RICHARD MORDEN

A HIGH FIVE TO

ANH
DO

FOR REMINDING US OF
THE BRIGHT SIDE TO LIFE

Here's a
shout-out to
all those who
overcome
hardship and
build themselves
a joyous future.

ANH DO

(1977-)

Anh Do is a much-loved comedian, author and artist. As a child, he and his family were forced to escape persecution in post-war Vietnam. They fled in an nine-metre fishing boat – which was attacked by pirates twice – and stayed in a refugee camp in Malaysia before arriving in Australia.

Growing up poor, Anh's dream was simple: get a job and buy his mother a house. Aged 23 he had the pleasure of doing just that. He had been saving money since high school – first from selling pet fish, then running market stalls.

He studied law and began experimenting with stand-up comedy. Audiences were won over by Anh's genuine, friendly manner and great storytelling, and he left law behind.

With his comedy career established, Anh wrote a candid memoir detailing the hardships his family had faced and showing us a side of refugees we too rarely get to hear about. *The Happiest Refugee* became an award-winning bestseller. Merging his knack for humour and spinning a yarn, Anh has gone on to write more than a dozen books for young readers.

So … successful stand-up comedian. Bestselling author. How about acclaimed artist? Anh's paintings have been finalists in the Archibald Prize and he has hosted the interview and portrait series *Anh's Brush with Fame*.

What's next? Anh has no major life plan, living by his father's ethos: 'There are only two times in life: now and too late.'

Anh, your positivity, talent and work ethic are remarkable.

We want to bring as much happiness to the world as you do.

ILLUSTRATION BY BENJAMIN CONSTANTINE

A HIGH FIVE TO

ARCHIE ROACH

FOR SHARING HIS
SONGS AND HIS STORY

Let's stop
and listen to
the songwriters
and storytellers
who have
something
important to
say about
our world.

ARCHIE ROACH

(1956-)

Archie Roach is a singer and songwriter whose career spans decades. He is a member of the Stolen Generations, having been taken from his family by the authorities when he was very young. He was fostered by a family in Melbourne who taught him to play piano and guitar. But being stolen from his family meant Archie had few ties to his Aboriginal heritage and no knowledge of his birth parents.

When Archie was a young man, an older sister wrote and explained how they had been taken and their family torn apart. Devastated and angry, Archie grabbed his guitar and ran away to seek answers. Through a period of homelessness and depression, Archie began performing and singing with Ruby Hunter, another member of the Stolen Generations, whom he would later marry and raise a family with.

Archie's debut solo album, *Charcoal Lane*, focused on his experiences and injustices and was a huge success, leading to tours around Australia and internationally and further albums.

As impressive as Archie's discography is, he also shines as a human rights spokesperson and activist. From winning a Human Rights Achievement Award for his song 'Took the Children Away' (the first time a songwriter had received the honour) to establishing the Archie Roach Foundation (a charity that aims to empower young people through the arts), he hasn't rested on his musical laurels. He's even opened his home to Indigenous youths dealing with the same kinds of issues he once faced.

Archie, you've moved and informed so many people through your music and generosity.

We want to respect and listen to the stories that each of us has to tell.

ILLUSTRATION BY GREGG DREISE

A HIGH FIVE TO

BANJO PATERSON

FOR HELPING SHAPE
AUSTRALIA'S HISTORY

Sing loud and long for the bush balladeers who bring the outback to life with their words and songs.

BANJO PATERSON

(1864-1941)

Andrew Barton 'Banjo' Paterson was many things: soldier, war correspondent, editor, poet, writer and Australian cultural icon.

He was born into a settler family in country New South Wales, where his love and respect for bush life grew. When he was ten years old he was sent to live with his grandmother to finish his education in Sydney, where he eventually worked as a lawyer.

City life wasn't for Banjo – he missed the bush. So with his passion for poetry he decided to write stories and poems that brought the bush to the city. In 1885 he began submitting his work to the *Bulletin* under his famous pen name, 'Banjo', which was the name of his favourite racehorse as a boy. The nation fell in love with Banjo's simple stories and his romantic and heroic depictions of swagmen, bushrangers, drovers and shearers, set among Australia's amazing and unique landscapes.

In 1895 *The Man from Snowy River and Other Verses* was released and sold out in a week, breaking all publishing records in Australia. In that year he also wrote his most famous bush ballad, 'Waltzing Matilda', which is considered by some an unofficial national anthem.

Numerous adventures took him overseas, but after several stints working as a war correspondent, Banjo decided to return home and write full time. In 1939 Banjo was appointed Commander of the Order of the British Empire in recognition of his contribution to literature.

Banjo, your tales of outback Australia will always have a place in our hearts.

We'll come a-waltzin' Matilda with you!

ILLUSTRATION BY ANDREW WELDON

A HIGH FIVE TO

BEN QUILTY

FOR CREATING ARRESTING IMAGES

Let's stop to
admire the
men whose art
encourages us
to think deeply,
show compassion
and believe in
second chances.

BEN QUILTY

(1973-)

Ben Quilty was passionate about art from a young age. He spent hours drawing and painting in his room and his HSC artwork was included in the ARTEXPRESS exhibition at the Art Gallery of New South Wales.

Painting has taken Ben from artist residencies in Paris and Spain and exhibitions in London and Hong Kong to painting Australian Defence Force personnel in Afghanistan as an official war artist. Back in Australia, he created portraits of the families of personnel who were killed or injured in service to show the wider impacts of war.

Themes such as empathy, youthful mistakes and second chances recur in Ben's art. In 2016 he travelled to Europe and the Middle East with writer Richard Flanagan to document refugees who'd fled war-torn Syria. He also became a mentor to Myuran Sukumaran, an Australian convicted of drug trafficking in Indonesia. He advocated for Myuran to escape the death penalty, saying that although Myuran was guilty, he had reformed and deserved another chance.

Ben has won numerous awards for his work. One of his best known pieces is his portrait of the late artist Margaret Olley, for which he won the Archibald Prize in 2011. It features broad strokes of impasto and paint, building up to thick, textured layers. Ben shows Margaret as an elderly woman, and although her face is loosely drawn it is incredibly expressive, full of curiosity and life. This compassion for his subjects, combined with his imagination and technical skill, is what makes Ben's work so exciting and powerful.

Ben, your art is thought-provoking, emotive and so wonderful to look at.

We hope to see the world as clearly and humanely as you do.

ILLUSTRATION BY MULGA

A HIGH FIVE TO

BOB BROWN

FOR SPEAKING UP AND
REFUSING TO BACK DOWN

A big
tree-hugging
thanks to the
community
representatives
who lobby
tirelessly for
social issues.

BOB BROWN

(1944-)

Bob Brown trained in medicine and worked as a doctor in Australia and England before settling in Tasmania. He became a leader in the state's conservation movement and in 1972 he joined the United Tasmania Group. It was the world's first 'green' or environmentally motivated political party.

In 1982 he joined the Parliament of Tasmania as an Independent – but he had a most unusual start. Just before he was appointed, he had been arrested while protesting against the potentially devastating (and eventually abandoned) Franklin Dam development.

Bob helped create the Tasmanian Greens and campaigned for issues such as saving Tasmania's ancient forests. He turned to Federal politics in 1996 and co-founded the Australian Greens. He led the party from 2005 until his retirement in 2012. In parliament he supported many environmental and human rights issues, including blocking radioactive waste dumping, championing asylum seeker rights, opposing the Iraq War in 2003 and advocating for alternative energy technologies. He was the first openly gay member of the Parliament of Australia and the first openly gay senator. The Australian Greens remain an important representative party in politics today.

Since resigning from parliament, Bob has been involved in various non-profit organisations focusing on environmental conservation. Throughout his life he's received several awards for his dedication to environmental causes and for excelling in his civic duty.

Bob, we're grateful for your bravery, your commitment and your campaigning for the future of this country.

We vote for engagement in political issues.

ILLUSTRATION BY TOHBY RIDDLE

A HIGH FIVE TO
BRIGGS
FOR HIS BLISTERING CREATIVITY

Turn up the volume for the hot-shot artists driving social change.

BRIGGS

(1986-)

Adam Briggs grew up in Shepparton, Victoria. He's a Yorta Yorta man with many talents, including music, acting and comedy writing.

Check it . . . Briggs began his music career as a solo rapper, receiving high accolades for his work including Album of the Year at the National Indigenous Music Awards in 2015. That same year he started the record label Bad Apples Music, which supports Aboriginal and Torres Strait Islander artists.

Briggs is also one half of the acclaimed hip-hop duo A.B. Original. Their music aims to bring conversations about Indigenous Australia to the forefront. Their award-winning first album, *Reclaim Australia*, covers subjects affecting Indigenous people such as youth incarceration, racism, deaths in custody and issues with health and life expectancy. The song 'January 26', featuring Dan Sultan, has become a popular anthem for both Indigenous and non-Indigenous Australians calling for the date of Australia Day to be changed due to the historical significance of the date for First Nations people.

Briggs's talent doesn't stop there. He has a successful TV career as a writer and cast member for several Australian comedy shows including *Black Comedy*, *Get Krack!n* and *The Weekly with Charlie Pickering*, and he appeared in the drama *Cleverman*. He's also part of the writing team for an upcoming American animated show from the creator of *The Simpsons*, Matt Groening.

Briggs, your creativity, honesty and sense of humour have made you an entertainer to watch and admire.

Your beat inspires us.

ILLUSTRATION BY BRENTON McKENNA

A HIGH FIVE TO

CHRIS RILEY

FOR HIS COMPASSION
AND DETERMINATION

Here's to the
men who believe
in the good in
people and bring
out their best.

CHRIS RILEY

(1954–)

Christopher Keith Riley was born and grew up in Victoria, on a dairy farm. He left school in 1973 and was driven to become a teacher after seeing the 1938 movie *Boys Town*, about a priest who established a school for socially disadvantaged boys.

Chris studied theology and was ordained as a priest in 1982. In the following years Father Chris worked as a teacher, youth worker and probation officer, as well as obtaining qualifications in sociology, counselling, Aboriginal Studies and psychology. He worked in a home for disadvantaged kids in Sydney, but wanted to find a way to help the children he saw struggling with homelessness.

In 1991 he founded a charity for disadvantaged youth, Youth Off the Streets. He began with one van, providing free meals and a friendly ear to homeless youths in the city. Since then, the non-denominational charity has expanded across New South Wales and runs international relief projects too. It oversees more than 20 early intervention and prevention programs to help young people who have survived trauma, abuse and neglect.

Father Chris was appointed a Member of the Order of Australia and received an Australian Human Rights Medal in 2006. His driving force is that no child is born bad, but that difficult family situations, environments or circumstances can have adverse effects on children and teens. He steadfastly encourages us to have 'the courage to demand greatness from our youth'.

Father Chris, your faith in the ability of young people to overcome adversity has improved so many lives.

We admire your dedication.

ILLUSTRATION BY LACHLAN CONN

A HIGH FIVE TO
COSENTINO
FOR DREAMING BIG

Prepare to be
amazed by the
mind-boggling
magicians
who constantly
challenge our
notions of what
is possible.

COSENTINO

(1982–)

As a child, Paul Cosentino was a far cry from the confident cool cat he is today. Back then he was shy and not the most popular kid at school. He struggled with reading and writing, so it's fair to say the library wasn't his favourite hangout. Yet it was during a visit to the library with his mum that he stumbled across a book about magic. HEY PRESTO! Cosentino had found his true passion in life. That book not only inspired him to keep reading, it propelled him on a truly magical journey.

After years of practise to hone his illusion skills, Cosentino's big break came in 2011 when he was runner-up on the reality show *Australia's Got Talent*. Week after week, he entertained and baffled the nation with his jaw-dropping performances and daring escape acts.

Since then he has gone on to wow the world with international tours and top-rating TV specials, which have been broadcast in more than 40 countries. In 2013 he not only won *Dancing with the Stars*, he also received the coveted Merlin Award for 'International Magician of the Year' – not bad for a shy kid who dreamed big!

Cosentino's success doesn't stop there. Inspired by his own personal struggle with learning difficulties – and with the hope of encouraging kids to delve into reading and unlock their imaginations – he has co-authored the fantasy book series *The Mysterious World of Cosentino*.

Cosentino, you have proven that with passion and perseverance, anything is possible.

We can't wait to see what else you've got up your sleeve!

ILLUSTRATION BY BENJAMIN CONSTANTINE

A HIGH FIVE TO

CRAIG REUCASSEL

FOR THE LAUGHS
AND THE INSIGHT

A thundering
roar of
appreciation
for those who
make us laugh
and make
us think.

CRAIG REUCASSEL

(1976-)

Craig Reucassel grew up in country New South Wales and has gone on to make quite a name for himself around Australia — and yet he still seems like the boy next door.

While he was studying economics and law at the University of Sydney, Craig and some of his fellow classmates formed the satirical comedy group The Chaser, named after the newspaper they had started in 1999. Their sense of humour and focus on current affairs and politics made the Australian Broadcasting Corporation take notice, and by 2001 they had their first TV show, *The Election Chaser*. They went on to make many more very funny and popular TV shows — although sometimes their stunts caused controversy! In between working with The Chaser team, Craig has co-hosted a radio show, performed in plays, and presented on the consumer affairs show *The Checkout*.

Most recently, Craig made the whole nation think about our habits when he hosted a documentary called *War on Waste*. Craig showed us how much food the average Australian family wastes each week, how the disposable coffee cups we chuck out add up, where our plastic bags end up, the problems that fast fashion trends can cause, and how a few simple changes at home and at our supermarkets can cut Australia's waste dramatically.

Craig, you inspire us to be better and take action to help the planet, and that makes you a hero in our eyes.

We raise our reusable coffee cups to you!

A HIGH FIVE TO

DAVID McALLISTER

FOR LEAPING
FORWARD

Let's give a standing ovation to the talented performers who follow their passion and challenge stereotypes.

DAVID McALLISTER

(1963–)

After seeing a television documentary on the famous ballet dancer Rudolf Nureyev, seven-year-old David McAllister was hooked. He had always been a bit of a performer, and now he wanted to dance. First, David had to convince his parents to let him take lessons. After clearing that hurdle with a grand jeté he had to face his schoolmates, and even some of his teachers, who didn't think that boys should dance.

David met disapproval and bullying with unwavering passion and commitment. He continued his ballet lessons and joined The Australian Ballet in 1983. Just six years later he was made a principal artist in the company. He danced many principal roles, including those in *The Sleeping Beauty*, *Don Quixote* and *Coppélia*. Despite his success, David faced criticism for not having the traditional physique of a lead male dancer. He carried on, determined to prove his critics wrong.

In 2001 David was named the Artistic Director of The Australian Ballet. Under David's leadership, the company has upheld the classical beauty of the art while showcasing a contemporary edge that delights audiences of all ages.

David has challenged the traditional body type expected of the company's dancers, pushing for a wider variety of shapes to be embraced. He also fought for dancers to have a life outside ballet and has championed women returning to the company after having children. It is no surprise then that David was awarded a Medal of the Order of Australia in 2004 for his services to ballet.

David, you were born to dance and have helped make an exclusive world more accessible for others.

We demand an encore!

ILLUSTRATION BY LACHLAN CONN

A HIGH FIVE TO
DAVID WALSH
FOR HIS VISION

Raise your glass
to the aficionados
who share their
passions and
creativity with
the world.

DAVID WALSH

(1961–)

A gambler who abhors pokies, David Walsh has never been one to follow convention. David grew up in Glenorchy, one of the poorest suburbs in Tasmania. An academically gifted student, he studied maths and computer science at university. In his second year, David designed a mathematical model that allowed him to win at blackjack in a local casino. Soon after this initial success, David dropped out of university to devote his time to developing the model's scope in order to win at other forms of gambling. David managed to beat the odds and became a multi-millionaire. We can't recommend his methods of making a fortune, since gambling is notorious for creating more losers than winners, but we can be impressed by how David went on to spend it.

David began collecting art when he purchased an old Yoruba palace door he had seen in an art gallery in Johannesburg, South Africa. This was the beginning of what would become a world-class collection of Roman, Hellenic and Egyptian artefacts. Realising that he needed somewhere to house his works, David decided to found a museum.

The Museum of Old and New Art (MONA) opened in January 2011. Since its launch, MONA has become one of Tasmania's foremost tourist attractions and draws visitors from all over the world. Like David, the museum's building, collections and exhibits are full of juxtapositions and contradictions which never cease to stir up the international art world.

David, we admire you for your ingenuity and for using your fortune to create something as unique as you are.

We're lucky to have you!

ILLUSTRATION BY BROLGA

A HIGH FIVE TO

DENG THIAK ADUT

FOR ASTONISHING TENACITY

Our thanks
to those who
transform their
own stories of
survival into
opportunities
for others.

DENG THIAK ADUT

When Deng Thiak Adut was about six years old, war came to his quiet village on the River Nile, in what is now South Sudan. Deng was taken from his family and conscripted into the Sudan People's Liberation Army as a child soldier. During this time he endured incredible hardships and witnessed the terrible atrocities of war.

A chance encounter reunited Deng with his brother John Mac. Risking his life, John smuggled Deng out of Sudan and managed to secure the two of them passage to Australia. On arrival Deng didn't speak English and had no idea about Western culture but, little by little, he built a future in his new country. Deng educated himself, studied determinedly and now holds a Master's Degree in Law and works as a criminal lawyer. In this role he focuses on serving Western Sydney where he grew up, including providing regular pro bono work for those who can't afford legal fees.

After a video of Deng's story went viral, Deng used his public profile to help people understand the horrors refugees face and to promote the importance of education. He gave the 2016 Australia Day address and was named the NSW Australian of the Year for 2017. Deng has also established a charity in the name of his brother who was killed in South Sudan in 2014. The John Mac Foundation works to support education and justice in Australia and South Sudan.

Deng, your powerful story and your work are helping so many in need.

We thank you for your advocacy.

ILLUSTRATION BY TOHBY RIDDLE

A HIGH FIVE TO

DOUGLAS MAWSON

FOR HIS COURAGE AND
ADVENTUROUS SPIRIT

A warm welcome
to the pioneers
who champion
curiosity and
discovery,
no matter
the challenges
they face.

DOUGLAS MAWSON

(1882-1958)

Sir Douglas Mawson led the first Australian expedition to Antarctica. He originally travelled to the ice-covered continent in 1907 with English explorer Ernest Shackleton, where he was one of the first humans to reach the vicinity of the South Magnetic Pole.

Douglas's Australian expedition left Hobart on 2 December 1911 on the *Aurora*. He and his team built their main base at the place they named Commonwealth Bay — now known as the windiest place on Earth. With two other scientists, Xavier Mertz and Belgrave Edward Sutton Ninnis, Douglas set off to explore previously unknown parts of the continent. He drew maps, logged the location of glaciers and collected rock samples and other scientific data.

The journey was difficult and, tragically, Mertz and Ninnis both perished. Douglas trekked the last 160 kilometres back to the base alone, with limited food and water supplies. When he finally made it, the *Aurora* had left without him to avoid being trapped in ice. Fortunately, several crew had remained behind as the search party and they all soon returned to Australia.

In 1914 Mawson was knighted for his work in the Antarctic and later awarded the Order of the British Empire. Mawson's account of his amazing journey was published in his book *The Home of the Blizzard* and his team's significant research was detailed in 22 scientific journals. Experts considered it one of the greatest polar expeditions because of the detailed observations made and because the team was the first to transmit weather data from Antarctica to Melbourne via radio.

Douglas, your survival in the face of extreme challenges is inspiring.

We applaud your contribution to scientific research.

ILLUSTRATION BY MULGA

A HIGH FIVE TO

EDDIE AYRES

FOR HIS MUSIC AND HIS VOICE

Please give
a round of
applause for the
men who share
their knowledge
and stories so
that other people
can feel a little
less alone.

EDDIE AYRES

(1967–)

Eddie Ayres has taken some long and difficult paths in life. Born in England, he studied music in Manchester, London and Berlin. He played classical viola professionally for 12 years and hosted radio programs in Hong Kong and Australia. He even cycled solo for nine months from England to Hong Kong. He published a memoir and spoke at conferences about the way music influences our emotions. He moved to Afghanistan to teach children music, while the country and its people attempted to recover from years of war and repressive rule.

Despite these and other accomplishments, Eddie also experienced terrible unease – about who he was, how people saw him and how they thought he ought to be. For much of his life, Eddie was known as Emma and lived as a woman, but the label and expectations didn't feel right. He had known for years that he was a transgender man, but tried to push the thought away because he was anxious that speaking up could mean losing his family, friends and career. Denying who he was put huge pressure on Eddie, leaving him unhappy. Gradually he accepted himself and began to let the people in his life know that 'Emma' was really Eddie.

Since then, Eddie has returned to Australia, published a second memoir and returned to hosting on ABC radio. He's said that he tries not to regret waiting so long to accept himself. Now is the time to focus on living the best way he can.

Eddie, thank you for sharing your insight, wit and voice – both when it comes to music and being true to oneself.

We know you have given others hope.

ILLUSTRATION BY TOM JELLETT

A HIGH FIVE TO

EDDIE WOO

FOR MAKING A DIFFERENCE IN THE CLASSROOM AND BEYOND

Full marks to
the teachers
and mentors who
inspire us
to keep learning
and striving.

EDDIE WOO

(1985–)

The school years weren't always happy for Eddie Woo – he experienced racism and bullying, and during high school he took charge of caring for his mother when she became unwell.

Despite his tough experiences, Eddie excelled at school and had his pick of subjects at university. His family encouraged him to focus on a career in law or medicine – but Eddie had other ideas. He wanted to give something back and make a difference in the very place that helped shape him. So he became a maths teacher, even though the subject hadn't always come naturally to him. Eddie used his own experiences, compassion and infectious enthusiasm to relate to students.

In 2012 a student of Eddie's was diagnosed with cancer and had to spend time away from school. Eddie decided to help the student feel included by recording his classes and putting them on YouTube. What started as an act of empathy quickly became a viral sensation. Soon other students were clamouring to watch the recorded lessons – first kids from his school and then students from around Australia and overseas. Eddie now has more than 200,000 subscribers engaging in his classes and shows us we can do more than 'just get by' in mathematics.

Students aren't the only ones who admire Eddie. He's received numerous awards and honours, including being a joint recipient of the 2015 NSW Premier's Prize for Innovation in Science and Mathematics Education and Local Hero in the 2018 Australia Day Awards.

Eddie, you remind us to 'Like' all the passionate teachers who make a huge difference to students.

We want to inspire and excite the way you do.

ILLUSTRATION BY CHRIS NIXON

A HIGH FIVE TO

ELVIS ABRAHANOWICZ

FOR SHARING HIS
TASTY TALENT

Bon appétit
to the marinaters
and barbecuers
for keeping
our tastebuds
excited.

ELVIS ABRAHANOWICZ

(1980-)

Elvis Abrahanowicz is one of the most exciting chefs and restaurateurs in Australia. Along with his wife, maître d' and stylist Sarah Doyle, friend and co-chef Ben Milgate, and other business partners, Elvis is the co-owner of numerous establishments in Sydney, including Porteño and Bodega. He also publishes regular recipes in magazines and newspapers.

Born in Argentina, Elvis was seven when his family immigrated to Western Sydney. He grew up with weekend family barbecues and was surrounded by the tradition of sharing food. When he opened his own restaurant, heritage was an important part of the ethos of the business, and his parents are still part of his kitchen staff.

His restaurants champion South American dishes and use Argentinian *asado* (barbecue) techniques and *parrilla* grills. Following the motto 'a full belly means a happy heart', Elvis's restaurants encourage diners to share dishes and experience diversity in food with a focus on fresh, local and seasonal produce.

Elvis and Ben Milgate were co-winners of *The Sydney Morning Herald Good Food Guide* Chef of the Year in 2012. They are sometimes referred to as the 'Surry Hillbillies' because of their rockabilly look and love of all things from the 1950s era – music, cars and style. His venues are known for beautiful design, lively music and a cosy atmosphere. Elvis's passion for vibrant dining experiences extends to collaboration in a growing range of food businesses run by former employees, colleagues and friends.

Elvis, your skill, style and entrepreneurial sense are the best ingredients for a mouth-watering meal.

Let's turn up the heat on fun experiences with food!

ILLUSTRATION BY JAMES GULLIVER HANCOCK

A HIGH FIVE TO

HAMISH AND ANDY

FOR BEING OUR FUNNIEST MATES

A round of
applause to
the comedians
and performers
who bring
laughter and
friendship into
our lives.

HAMISH AND ANDY

(both 1981-)

Funnymen Hamish Blake and Andy Lee met as students at the University of Melbourne. Twelve months later, they'd landed their first radio show. They've been taking us along for an incredible ride ever since with their conversational, muck-around style that makes us feel like we're part of their family.

They've written for and appeared on shows such as *Rove*, *Spicks and Specks*, *The Project* and more. But it's their own personal content that we love so much. On radio, *The Hamish and Andy Show* achieved unparalleled success, injecting fun into the lives of more than two million listeners. Via radio and TV, they've taken us on their adventures — together we've sailed a tall ship to Tasmania, caravanned around Australia, found 'Australia's best bloke', taken a gap year all over the world, and shared our true stories with them too.

Lots of comedians depend on cutting wit but Hamish and Andy have always had a different style. Their relaxed humour and dedicated friendship stands out for both audiences and critics. They've won numerous Australian Commercial Radio Awards, ARIA Awards for their compilation albums, and finished their radio careers (for now) with a sell-out crowd of over 6000 people who turned up to watch them perform a single song.

Hamish and Andy, you've proven yourselves to be genuinely warm, kind, funny people.

You inspire us to strive for the same!

ILLUSTRATION BY ANDREW WELDON

HAMISH & ANDY

FAMISHED & DANDY

DANISH & BANDY

RAKISH & HANDY

CRAYFISH & SANDY

HAMMISH & ANDES

A HIGH FIVE TO

HARLEY WINDSOR

FOR HIS GRACE, DETERMINATION AND DRIVE

Tens across
the board for
the athletes
who dare to
dream big.

HARLEY WINDSOR

(1996–)

Harley Windsor's story is one of firsts. The 21-year-old from Rooty Hill became Australia's first Indigenous Winter Olympian at the 2018 Winter Olympics in Pyeongchang, South Korea.

Harley came to ice-skating by a fortunate wrong turn. His mother drove past the now-closed Blacktown ice rink in Sydney's west and Harley decided to give it a go. He loved it so much he couldn't stay away and soon started private lessons.

As Harley's style developed, it became clear that he was suited to pair skating, so his coaches found him a partner in Russian-born Ekaterina (Katia) Alexandrovskaya, who was a perfect match in technique and bodyline. The pair began training together in Moscow and Sydney and soon took the skating world by storm.

In 2016 the pair placed eighth overall at the International Skating Union (ISU) Junior Grand Prix in the Czech Republic. This was their international debut and just a hint of what was to come. In the same year, Harley and Katia won Australia's first ISU Junior Grand Prix gold medal in Tallinn, Estonia. They made headlines again by becoming the first Australian skaters to qualify for the ISU Junior Grand Prix Final. Other notable achievements include a historic win at the 2017 World Junior Championships in Taipei City.

Coming from a big family, at times Harley struggled with the isolation of living and training in a foreign country far from home. But with his parents' support, Harley found the courage to keep chasing his figure-skating dream.

Harley, we're proud of you for never giving up, and your prowess on the ice leaves us awestruck!

Keep going for gold!

ILLUSTRATION BY DAVID HARDY

A HIGH FIVE TO

HARRY SEIDLER

FOR COMBINING FUNCTION AND BEAUTY

Here's to the
creative and
innovative folk
who make our
environment
intriguing.

HARRY SEIDLER

(1923–2006)

Harry Seidler was born in Vienna but fled to England as a teenager after Austria was occupied by Nazi Germany. Soon after, he was interned by the British authorities as an enemy alien and sent to Canada. On his release he studied architecture and so began a lifelong passion for turning buildings into works of art.

Harry came to Australia in 1948 when his parents, who had migrated to Sydney two years before, commissioned him to design their family home. His bold design, inspired by his Bauhaus-influenced training, was unconventional in Australia and combined art, architecture and technology. Soon, Rose Seidler House (named after his mother) was 'the most talked about house in Sydney'. The building launched Harry's career and convinced him to stay in Australia, and influenced a new wave of modern design in the country.

As time passed and building technology changed, so did Harry's architectural style. Keen to embrace new techniques and possibilities, he shaped concrete into sweeping curves in buildings such as Australia Square Tower and Horizon Apartments, and transformed steel into waves for the Ian Thorpe Aquatic Centre.

Ever sharply dressed in his trademark bow tie, Harry continued to design iconic and innovative Australian buildings and residences into his eighties. He received numerous honours in his lifetime, including Companion of the Order of Australia and Officer of the Order of the British Empire.

Harry, you created beautiful buildings and brought an international flair to Australian shores.

We stand in awe of your buildings.

ILLUSTRATION BY TOHBY RIDDLE

A HIGH FIVE TO
HOWARD FLOREY
FOR BREAKING THE MOULD

Thanks are not enough for the stalwart scientists whose curiosity and dedication advance medical research and improve our health.

HOWARD FLOREY

(1898–1968)

From an early age, Howard Florey was academically brilliant. He studied at Adelaide and Oxford universities, but few could have imagined the impact of his future achievements.

In 1938 Howard was a professor at the Sir William Dunn School of Pathology at the University of Oxford. One lazy afternoon, Howard was indulging in a spot of 'light reading', leafing through some back issues of *The British Journal of Experimental Pathology*. He stumbled upon Alexander Fleming's paper on the penicillium mould. This got the cogs in Howard's brain turning. He had long been interested in the ways that bacteria and mould naturally kill each other and he decided that he – and his team of awesome scientists – were going to unravel the science behind Fleming's famous fungus.

By 1940 Howard and his talented team had managed to isolate the active ingredient of the penicillium mould juice, purify it and figure out which germs it was effective against. After countless setbacks, tests and trials the world's first antibiotic, penicillin, had been created.

Thanks to Howard and his team, large-scale production of penicillin was developed. This came at a critical time towards the end of World War II, saving the lives of injured forces, and millions of lives since. In 1945 this monumental achievement was honoured when Howard, along with Ernst B. Chain and Alexander Fleming, received the Nobel prize for Physiology or Medicine for their contribution in bringing penicillin to the world.

Howard, you revolutionised medical science and will forever be an inspiration to young scientists.

We are in awe of your inquisitive mind.

ILLUSTRATION BY DANIEL GRAY-BARNETT

A HIGH FIVE TO

HUGH
JACKMAN

FOR BEING TRUE BLUE

Bravo to the
chameleon
performers
who entertain
us and show us
other lives
and worlds.

HUGH JACKMAN

(1968-)

Hugh Jackman was the youngest of five children and raised in Sydney by his father. Though he fell in love with the theatre in high school, it wasn't until he was finishing university that he started to pursue his passion for performance.

Hugh says he felt like a dunce compared to other students while studying drama – but that gave him the drive to work extra hard. Soon after finishing intensive acting training, he won the lead role in the ABC TV series *Correlli*, then showed his versatility by singing and dancing in stage musicals. His big break was super-hero level big: playing Wolverine in the *X-Men* franchise, followed by roles in *Kate & Leopold*, *Van Helsing*, *The Prestige*, *Australia* and *Les Misérables*. On stage, he played iconic Australian singer-songwriter Peter Allen in *The Boy from Oz,* for which he won a Tony award.

It's not all glitz and fame, though – Hugh and his wife, actor and producer Deborra-lee Furness, are known for working to make their Hollywood life as balanced and normal as possible. Hugh prioritises family time, and never spends more than a fortnight away from his children and wife. He may play tough guys, but on set, he makes a point of making friends with those he interacts with – from co-stars to the crew. That interest in and care for others spills out into charity work too – Hugh has donated money and time to a number of charity organisations including Charity: Water, Operation of Hope, Global Poverty Project, World Vision and many more.

Hugh, you've flown high without ever losing sight of the importance of kindness and generosity.

We'll be watching whatever you do next!

ILLUSTRATION BY DAVID HARDY

A HIGH FIVE TO

JACK
MUNDEY

FOR DARING TO
MAKE A STAND

Let's wave our banners for the leaders and activists who help make our cities and towns liveable and lovely for those from all walks of life.

JACK MUNDEY

(1929–)

Jack Mundey was born in Malanda, in far north Queensland, in 1929. As a young man he came to Sydney, where he played football professionally and then began work as a labourer. He became active in the union movement, and was appointed secretary of the New South Wales branch of the Builders Labourers Federation from 1968 to 1975.

During the 1970s, the skyline of Sydney was rapidly changing; massive skyscrapers, luxury apartments and shopping precincts were new features of the urban environment. But some felt that this development came at a cost, with the city losing its open spaces, public housing and environmental and historical heritage. In response, Jack and many labourers refused to work on building projects they thought were socially undesirable or irresponsible. In contrast to traditional union 'black bans' on unsafe or poorly managed projects, Jack coined the term 'green bans' to refer to these strike actions, because their aim was to protect the natural and built environment.

The most lasting impacts of the Green Ban movement can be seen in inner-city Sydney, where Jack and union and community members fought to preserve significant sites in the historic Rocks area, Centennial Park and Victoria Street in Kings Cross. In the decades since the height of the Green Bans, Jack has remained at the forefront of the fight to protect the city as a place for the many, not the few; and for the planet, not the profiteers.

Jack, your commitment to political advocacy and environmentalism is legendary, and has had an enduring influence on the way we think about cities, heritage and conservation.

Thank you for fighting the good fight!

ILLUSTRATION BY ANDREW JOYNER

A HIGH FIVE TO

JASON BALL

FOR CELEBRATING PRIDE

Raise a flag for
the guys who
use honesty and
compassion to
speak out and
make the world
a little more
welcoming
for everyone.

JASON BALL

(1988–)

Growing up in regional Victoria, Jason Ball was a footy fan from a young age – he loved playing it, watching it, talking about it. On the cusp of becoming a teenager Jason realised he was gay but, unlike footy, this wasn't something he wanted to talk about. Afraid of what his friends and family might think, Jason tried to push it aside. However, once he found someone to talk to, he began the process of accepting himself and opening up to his family and friends.

Fast-forward to 2012, when Jason became the first Australian Rules footballer at any level to come out as gay in the national media. He then started advocating for inclusion and diversity in the game, which led to the creation of the AFL Pride Game, which has been played since 2016. Alongside his anti-homophobia work in sport, Jason has also taken up ambassadorial roles for beyondblue and the Safe Schools Coalition Australia, speaking to thousands about issues of sexuality and mental health.

Although at first he wasn't comfortable with flying the rainbow flag, Jason's passion and drive comes from his strong belief that having a role model in the public eye will make a difference to the people who need it most. In 2016 Jason also took a stand on other issues, running as a candidate for the Greens and campaigning on climate change, support for asylum seekers, science, mental health and marriage equality.

Jason, your courage has paved the way for a more inclusive society, not just in sport but in schools, workplaces and day-to-day life too.

We want to wave the rainbow flag with you!

ILLUSTRATION BY MATTHEW MARTIN

A HIGH FIVE TO

JOHN CURTIN

FOR NEVER BACKING DOWN

A nod to our
political leaders
who have the
smarts to govern
and the courage
to see their
decisions through.

JOHN CURTIN

(1885-1945)

After a long association with the Australian Labor Party – and despite a personal struggle with alcohol addiction – John Curtin became the 14th Prime Minister of Australia in October 1941. Two months later Japan attacked the United States of America's Pacific naval base in Hawaii. This immediately drew Australia into the Pacific front of World War II. Japanese military forces occupied most of South-East Asia and continued to press southward. No one thought they would stop at Australia's coastline.

Most Australian troops were serving overseas in the Middle East. Curtin insisted that Britain's Prime Minister, Winston Churchill, return the Australian 7th Division to defend Australia. It was a courageous and unprecedented move, which ultimately secured the country against invasion.

Curtin was also a great supporter of social policy. Under his government, pensions and welfare services were expanded to help a wide range of disadvantaged people. He supported wage equality for working women and implemented new policies to assist our First Nations' peoples. When it came to fairness and justice he always seemed to be way ahead of the game.

Through all of this his physical health was never good and on 5 July 1945, with the end of the war against Japan in sight, he died from heart disease. He had his critics, even at the time of his death, but he was also mourned by many Australians who appreciated his compassion for others.

John, you battled your demons and worked to make Australia a fairer country.

We hope all our leaders can have your insight and courage!

ILLUSTRATION BY HARRY SLAGHEKKE

A HIGH FIVE TO

JOHN FLYNN

FOR BRIDGING THE LONGEST DISTANCES

Let's remember
the innovators
who use
kindness and
determination to
create change
and to help
develop our
great nation!

JOHN FLYNN

(1880-1951)

John Flynn was born in Victoria and from an early age he was interested in a wide range of subjects. Unable to afford university, he instead studied theology and was ordained in 1911. One of his first jobs was to travel to remote areas of Victoria and South Australia and report on living conditions. He did this for both the Indigenous and non-Indigenous communities and quickly realised that there was a desperate need for easier access to medical assistance. Sometimes people had to travel for hours or even days to get help if they were injured or sick! John was instrumental in establishing many bush hospitals in these communities and this changed people's lives for the better.

After receiving a letter from a young pilot serving in World War I, he was inspired to use aeroplanes to connect doctors and patients. It took years of campaigning and fundraising, but the result was the organisation known today as the Royal Flying Doctor Service. Advancements in radio technology eventually helped the service to grow nationally, with medical staff being able to communicate with patients and pilots. John was appointed an Officer of the Order of the British Empire in 1933.

John passed away in 1951, but his face might still be familiar to you – he's on the twenty-dollar note!

John, thanks for your commitment to improving lives in remote communities and for helping establish one of the most iconic services in Australia.

Your compassion will not be forgotten!

ILLUSTRATION BY TOM JELLETT

A HIGH FIVE TO

JOHNATHAN THURSTON

FOR KICKING MAJOR GOALS

Make some noise
for the men who
wear their colours
with pride and
use their renown
to change the
world for the
better.

JOHNATHAN THURSTON

(1983-)

Whenever rugby league superstar Johnathan Thurston's name is mentioned the phrase 'greatest player of all time' is never far away. Johnathan has captained the North Queensland Cowboys and is a representative in Australian international, Queensland State of Origin and Indigenous All Stars teams. He's also a four-time Dally M Medal winner and has the most career points in State of Origin to boot!

Surprisingly Johnathan was once the skinny kid that no footy team wanted. He trained and trained, waiting for his break, which eventually came at the Canterbury-Bankstown Bulldogs, where he made his NRL debut in 2002. After winning the Premiership with them in 2004, Johnathan moved back to his home state of Queensland to join the Cowboys.

During his rise to champion status, Johnathan has also had his struggles. In 2010, after the death of his uncle, Johnathan hit a low point and was arrested for a public nuisance offence. He says it was a wake-up call and led him to get in touch with his people and his culture.

Undoubtedly passionate about rugby league, Johnathan is now equally passionate about his family and his culture. A Gunggari man, he is a part of many initiatives that support Indigenous communities and is committed to inspiring the next generation of young Australians. Johnathan's work in this sector has been recognised with him being named the 2018 QLD Australian of the Year and being awarded the Australian Human Rights Medal.

Johnathan, you're a phenomenon on the field and fantastic role model off the field.

We see greatness in what you do.

ILLUSTRATION BY BRENTON McKENNA

A HIGH FIVE TO

JORDAN NGUYEN

FOR TRANSFORMING LIVES

We've sent a
time-machine
back from the
future to thank
those who use
technology
to empower
humanity.

JORDAN NGUYEN

As a teenager, Jordan Nguyen was keen to become a professional tennis player, but a back injury made him rethink his dream. Instead, he followed in his father's footsteps and studied engineering.

In his third year at university, Jordan was injured in a diving accident in a swimming pool. After his recovery, he dedicated himself to exploring technological innovations that could improve and transform people's lives. Jordan completed his PhD in Biomedical Engineering in 2012, drawing on his experience with spinal injury. He developed a mind-controlled wheelchair for people with high-level physical disability. This smart wheelchair not only has cameras and navigation assistance built in, but it is controlled by electrical energy in the operator's brain. It reads its user's thoughts!

Since that first invention, Dr Jordan Nguyen has been a man on a mission. He founded a social business, Psykinetic, to continue to create futuristic assistive technologies. He works with many organisations and groups to advocate for a more inclusive society and to improve the quality of life for people with disability. Best of all, this young genius shares his excitement about awesome new technologies and future possibilities with all of us through his talks, documentaries and TV presenting.

Jordan, your ideas are changing the world for the better, and the possibilities are endless.

We can't wait to see what you invent next.

A HIGH FIVE TO

KARL KRUSZELNICKI

FOR SHARING HIS
KNOWLEDGE

Put your hands
together for
the super sleek
geeks who make
science cool and
encourage us
to keep asking
questions.

KARL KRUSZELNICKI

(1948-)

Born in Sweden, Karl Kruszelnicki — better known as Dr Karl — immigrated to Australia with his family after World War II. He spent his early life in Bonegilla Migrant Reception Centre before the family settled in Wollongong.

Before he became the popular scientist we know today, he earned degrees in physics, biomedical engineering, medicine and surgery. He has worked as a physicist, tutor, filmmaker, car mechanic, labourer and medical doctor — that's a pretty impressive CV!

In 1981 Dr Karl decided to embark on a career in the media. He boldly walked into ABC radio station Double J (now Triple J) and offered to talk about the Space Shuttle launch — fortunately for him they agreed! Since then he has become one of Australia's most trusted sources of information.

For more than 30 years the science expert in the wacky shirts has indulged and encouraged the nation's curiosity. He has answered the most obscure scientific questions on radio, hosted television series including *Quantum* and *Sleek Geeks*, and authored (so far) 43 books covering pretty much every topic in the field of science.

In 2006 Dr Karl was made a Member of the Order of Australia. He is also the winner of the tongue-in-cheek Ig Nobel Prize for his work on belly button fluff, and is one of Australia's 100 National Living Treasures. He even has an asteroid named after him — Dr Karl/18412!

Dr Karl, your passion for knowledge and education
is totally infectious.

We can't wait to learn more!

ILLUSTRATION BY JAMES HART

A HIGH FIVE TO

KURT FEARNLEY

FOR PUSHING THE LIMITS

Let's cheer
for the sports
stars who defy
adversity, finding
the courage and
determination to
compete – and
win – against
all odds!

KURT FEARNLEY

(1981–)

When Kurt Fearnley was born, he was diagnosed with lumbar sacral agenesis, meaning he was missing the lower portion of his spine. Doctors thought he might survive for only a week. But even as a baby Kurt defied all odds.

Fast-forward 14 years and Kurt competed in his first race, on his school's grass oval in an everyday wheelchair. He was hooked. By the time he was 17 he was competing at an elite level in a specialised racing chair.

At 19 Kurt competed in the Sydney 2000 Summer Paralympic Games and in demonstration events at the Sydney 2000 Summer Olympics. He's competed at the Athens 2004, Beijing 2008, London 2012 and Rio de Janeiro 2016 Paralympics, and holds three gold, seven silver and three bronze medals.

But his superhuman feats are not confined to the wheelchair. In 2009 Kurt 'crawled' the gruelling 96 kilometre Kokoda Trail with his family to raise funds for Movember and beyondblue. He has also won the London, Paris, Seoul, Sydney, Chicago and New York marathons.

Kurt is a passionate disability advocate and teaches physical education in high schools around New South Wales. His feats on and off the sports field saw him awarded 2009 NSW Young Australian of the Year. In between teaching, training at the NSW Institute of Sport, meeting Queen Elizabeth II, advocacy work, and spending time with his wife and son, Kurt published an autobiography. Does this man have no limits?

Kurt, you're one of Australia's greatest athletes and an international legend.

We want to be as determined as you!

ILLUSTRATION BY JAMES FOSDIKE

A HIGH FIVE TO

MARK WESTMAN

FOR HELPING ANIMALS AND THEIR HUMANS

Raise your paws
for the generous
folk who donate
their time and
skills to make life
better for those
who are doing
it tough.

MARK WESTMAN

(1980-)

Dr Mark Westman loves animals. He trained for years to become a veterinarian, and has worked for over a decade at shelters such as the RSPCA and Animal Welfare League to help animals get healthy and ready for a second chance.

For many Australians, pets are like family. They give us companionship, someone to care for and – in the case of dogs – motivation to exercise, enjoy the outdoors and chat with the neighbours we see on our walks. Sadly, sometimes the people who need that companionship, purpose and friendly social interaction the most have the hardest time affording vet care for their pets.

So in 2009 Mark took a fold-out table and an esky of medication to a park. A local outreach program was giving assistance to homeless and disadvantaged people, and Mark offered free vet checks for the pets of the people attending. Pets in the Park Parramatta had begun.

Soon Mark was joined by vet nurses Vicki Cawsey and Linda Warlond and vet Dr Leah Skelsey to formally found Pets in the Park. The charity has expanded to other parts of Sydney, Melbourne, Brisbane and now Canberra to provide free health checks, vaccinations, flea and worm treatments, basic medication and donated pet food. It's helped hundreds of vulnerable people keep and care for their loyal mates.

We are so grateful to Mark and the Pets in the Park crew.

Dogs might be the best people, but we think you come pretty close.

ILLUSTRATION BY ANDREW JOYNER

A HIGH FIVE TO

MEI QUONG TART

FOR COMBINING
REMARKABLE BUSINESS
ACUMEN WITH GENEROSITY

Let's hear it for the men who turn challenges into opportunities for themselves and those around them.

MEI QUONG TART

(1850-1903)

Mei Quong Tart was born in Guangdong, China. As a nine-year-old he travelled with his uncle to the goldfields of colonial New South Wales. Quong, as he became known, was taken in by the Simpson family, who taught him English and gave him a share in a gold claim. By the time he was 21, Quong Tart was wealthy and well known for his involvement in local life.

In 1881 Quong Tart visited China to see his family and make connections for trade. When he returned to Australia, he set up silk and tea stores in Sydney, then opened the city's first tea rooms. These beautifully decorated restaurants became important meeting places, hosting high society as well as suffragette meetings and fundraisers for the poor and ill.

This mixture of grandeur and social conscience was typical of Quong Tart's life. He offered paid sick leave, holiday pay and personal leave for his employees, which was rare in those days. He campaigned against the opium trade and acted as an interpreter and advocate for Chinese immigrants at a time when fear and distrust of immigrants became a divisive political issue in New South Wales.

In 1886 he married English-born Margaret Scarlett, and they had two sons and four daughters. They lived in a grand home in Ashfield known as Gallop House, which now forms part of a nursing home. Today a statue in Ashfield honours Mei Quong Tart's memory.

Mei Quong Tart, we admire your resilience in adapting to a new country, your enterprise and your care for those less fortunate than yourself.

We remember your achievements.

ILLUSTRATION BY MATTHEW MARTIN

A HIGH FIVE TO

MICHAEL KIRBY

FOR FIGHTING THE GOOD FIGHT

Let's hear it for the legal eagles who dedicate their lives to the service of justice, leading the way to a better tomorrow.

MICHAEL KIRBY

(1939-)

After receiving a fine public education, Michael Kirby earned a Bachelor of Arts, a Bachelor of Laws, a Bachelor of Economics and Master of Laws from the University of Sydney. He became the youngest appointment to federal judicial office and worked his way up the ranks, culminating in his appointment to the High Court of Australia in 1996.

The running theme of Michael's legal career was his fearless, inquiring mind. He dared to challenge the status quo, despite the threat of controversy. He often voiced disagreement with his peers – so much so that he earned the nickname 'The Great Dissenter'. Over time, a number of his minority dissenting judgements become incorporated into the law.

Michael was the longest serving judge in Australia when he retired from the High Court in 2009, but his work was far from over. He supports a diverse range of causes, from the arts and public education, to human rights and animal protection. He is an advocate for LGBTQIA+ rights, and was the first openly gay judge in the High Court of Australia. After hanging up his black gown, Michael continued to work as an educator and as a jurist in the international sphere. He has served on UN commissions and panels, and received numerous accolades including the Australian Human Rights Medal, the UNESCO Prize for Human Rights Education, the Gruber Justice Prize and the Centenary Medal.

Michael, your unwavering commitment to championing human rights is inspiration for us all to never give up in the face of discrimination and injustice.

We aspire to be as dedicated as you.

ILLUSTRATION BY JAMES GULLIVER HANCOCK

A HIGH FIVE TO

MICK FANNING

FOR BEING A
TRUE CHAMPION

Awed applause
for the resilient
guys who achieve
awesome
physical feats
and get back
on their boards
after being
knocked off.

MICK FANNING

(1981–)

Mick Fanning learnt to surf at the age of five, but it wasn't until he was 12 and his family moved to northern New South Wales that he really started to focus on the sport. Before long he was carving his way up the Australian surfing scene, turning pro in 2002. The year ended on a high with Mick finishing in fifth position and being awarded the Association of Surfing Professionals (ASP) Rookie of the Year award.

Mick's surfing career suffered a near wipe-out in 2004 after a bad hamstring injury took surgery and six months of rehab to overcome. The hard work paid off in 2007 when Mick won the ASP World Title. He dedicated the win to his beloved brother who tragically passed away when Mick was 16. Mick then went on to win the 2009 and 2013 World Titles.

Mick is also known for his encounter with a shark during the J-Bay Open finals in Jeffreys Bay, South Africa, in 2015. He fought off the shark and made international headlines. But it's the way Mick uses his celebrity status out of the water that truly deserves to be front page news: among other things, he's an ambassador for the Starlight Children's Foundation and has made generous donations to shark attack victims. Mick's surfing achievements and charity work were recognised in 2017 with a Medal of the Order of Australia.

Mick, you've been through ups and downs both in and out of the water and have come out the end of the barrel with your head held high.

We want to give you a shaka, bro!

ILLUSTRATION BY TOM JELLETT

A HIGH FIVE TO

MIKE CANNON-BROOKES AND SCOTT FARQUHAR

FOR BREAKING
NEW GROUND

Upvotes to
the tech buffs
and savvy minds
who bring us the
tools we need for
the future.

MIKE CANNON-BROOKES AND SCOTT FARQUHAR

(both 1979-)

The enterprise software company Atlassian was founded by good mates Mike Cannon-Brookes and Scott Farquhar. The duo met at university and while they certainly weren't the highest achieving students, they formed a plan to create a company that sold software. They didn't know what kind of software but they realised that once it was developed, software could be replicated easily and sold over and over again via the internet. And so Atlassian, which builds collaboration and content management software, was born!

From humble beginnings running off a credit card debt and a staff of friends, Mike and Scott's company is now a billion-dollar enterprise.

Mike and Scott's Atlassian plan also extends to giving back. The company came up with the Pledge 1% movement: they donate 1% of annual profits, 1% of employee time, and 1% of company equity to helping make the world a better place through their Atlassian Foundation charity. The boys are now encouraging other companies to join the movement and have recently announced their new '10 million in 10 years' goal: to prepare 10 million disadvantaged youth for the workforce of the future within 10 years.

Mike and Scott, you've built something from nothing, brought an Australian start-up to the world stage and given back to those in need.

We aspire to do even half as much as you!

A HIGH FIVE TO

PAUL DE GELDER

FOR HIS COURAGE
AND RESILIENCE

Three cheers
for the daredevils
who don't let
fear and
adversity stand
in their way.

PAUL DE GELDER

(1977–)

Paul de Gelder was never one to shy away from a challenge. Drawn to danger and adventure, Paul worked as an army paratrooper before becoming an elite clearance diver with the Royal Australian Navy.

During a counter-terrorism exercise in Sydney Harbour in 2009, Paul was attacked by a bull shark. Paul fought off the shark but lost his right hand and the back of his right thigh. Fortunately the injuries weren't fatal but doctors had to amputate Paul's right forearm and leg.

Paul struggled through dark moments and excruciating pain. Despite this he found the strength to throw himself into his rehabilitation program. He was determined to get out of bed and moving again as soon as possible. Paul now has a prosthetic arm and leg and finds creative ways to maintain his mobility and independence.

After his recovery, Paul continued to instruct navy divers for another three and a half years before leaving the Navy to travel the world as a motivational speaker. He has also written a book about his experience and does talks and TV work to share his story and encourage others going through hard times. Paul is passionate about the environment and, despite his terrifying ordeal in the ocean, he has even spoken at the United Nations in favour of shark conservation.

Paul, you turned tragedy into triumph and your unbreakable spirit is truly inspiring.

We thank you for sharing your incredible story with the world!

ILLUSTRATION BY HARRY SLAGHEKKE

A HIGH FIVE TO

PAUL KELLY

FOR CELEBRATING
WHO WE ARE IN SONG

Let's hear it for the magnificent storytellers who capture the heart of Australia in their songs.

PAUL KELLY

(1955–)

A singer-songwriter, guitarist and harmonica player, Paul Kelly has worked solo and with many other artists and groups.

Paul was born in Adelaide. As a young man he travelled around Australia before settling in Melbourne in 1976. There he became involved in the pub rock scene and recorded two albums with his band, Paul Kelly and the Dots. Next stop was Sydney, where another band was formed and many hits were made.

Paul's songs have been critically acclaimed as well as top sellers. He has recorded more than 20 studio albums and many of his songs are now lodged deeply in the Australian psyche. His lyrics have a storytelling style, capturing aspects of Australian culture and the vastness of the landscape. He combines big themes with everyday details, plus characters and situations that feel familiar and real.

In 1997 Paul was inducted into the ARIA Hall of Fame. The Australasian Performing Rights Association (APRA) listed two of Paul's songs in the Top 30 Australian Songs of All time: 'To Her Door', and 'Treaty', which he co-wrote with members of Yothu Yindi. His collaboration with Kev Carmody, 'From Little Things Big Things Grow', describes the Gurindji Strike for Indigenous land rights, and is included in the National Film and Sound Archive's Sounds of Australia Registry. In 2017 Paul was appointed an Officer of the Order of Australia for service to the performing arts through his contributions as a singer, songwriter and musician.

Paul, you are a national treasure and a writing tour de force.

We hear ourselves in your music.

ILLUSTRATION BY BROLGA

A HIGH FIVE TO

PETER GRESTE

FOR SPEAKING OUT

Here's to the
men who don't
waver and whose
resolve can
change the world.

PETER GRESTE

(1965-)

Peter Greste grew up in Sydney and Brisbane. After high school, an exchange trip to South Africa sparked his interest in foreign affairs. He studied journalism and worked in Australia before moving overseas and becoming a freelance journalist for CNN, Reuters and the BBC.

After the September 11 attacks Peter covered the war in Afghanistan and worked all over the Middle East. He was based in Kenya, Africa from 2004 and received the prestigious Peabody Award for his documentary about life in war-torn Somalia.

In December 2013 Peter flew to Cairo, Egypt, to cover an unfolding political drama. This was part of the so-called 'Arab Spring', when citizens of many Middle Eastern nations took to the streets to overthrow unfair and authoritarian regimes. Peter's hotel room was raided by government agents, who arrested him and two fellow journalists. Peter and his colleagues were charged with spreading false news, and six months later were sentenced to seven years in jail. Finally, after an international outcry and a retrial, Peter was released and deported from Egypt in February 2015. He had spent 400 days in prison, all the while arguing that the charges against him were baseless and that his first trial had been a sham.

He now fights fiercely for press freedom of speech and advocates on behalf of silenced reporters around the world. He believes that journalists have a vital role in ensuring that governments are held to account, so that all people have the power to influence the decisions made on their behalf.

Peter, you've shown that dignity and resolute voices can win out.

We aim to be as steadfast as you.

ILLUSTRATION BY JAMES GULLIVER HANCOCK

A HIGH FIVE TO

SAMUEL JOHNSON

FOR BRINGING AWARENESS AND NEVER GIVING UP

Raise your hands
(and unicycles)
in honour of
those who strive
for medical
breakthroughs
and honour
the loved ones
they've lost.

SAMUEL JOHNSON

(1978–)

Samuel Johnson is an Australian actor, radio presenter, voiceover artist and philanthropist. As an actor Samuel is probably best known for his turn as Molly Meldrum in the miniseries *Molly* or as Evan in *The Secret Life of Us*. Both roles attracted awards from the Australian Film Institute and the Australian Academy of Cinema and Television Arts, and he won his very own Gold Logie.

Even so, where Samuel really shines is in his achievements as a philanthropist. When his sister, Connie, was diagnosed with cancer, Samuel threw himself into a personal campaign to make a real difference. Together, Samuel and Connie created the charity Love Your Sister to raise money and create further awareness of this all-too-common disease.

In 2013 Samuel began riding his unicycle on a nonstop journey around Australia. One year after setting off, he returned to Melbourne, having travelled 15,955 kilometres, raised more than $1.4 million in donations for much-needed research and with a Guinness World Record under his belt for good measure.

Samuel was awarded the Medal of the Order of Australia for services to cancer research support organisations in 2016, and he was the Victorian candidate for the 2018 Australian of the Year for his tireless and selfless efforts.

Sadly, Connie died in late 2017. In a moving interview on *The Project* Samuel declared that he would keep striving in her name to raise funds and fight breast cancer. It's hard to think of a better person to take on the good fight.

Samuel, we admire your perseverance and selflessness in the face of grief.

We hope to be as dedicated and strong as you.

ILLUSTRATION BY JAMES FOSDIKE

A HIGH FIVE TO
STEVE IRWIN
FOR BEING A WILDLIFE WARRIOR

A big 'crikey'
to the advocates
who champion
the preservation
and importance
of our wildlife.

STEVE IRWIN

(1962–2006)

Steve Irwin was devoted to all wildlife from a young age and grew up in the perfect environment for it – his parents owned a zoo in Queensland. He caught his first venomous snake aged six and would often help his dad capture crocodiles in populated areas and re-home them. His handling techniques and interest in reptiles led to his nickname – 'Crocodile Hunter'.

Once he met his wife, Terri, Steve began his career as a wildlife documentary maker, filming more than 150 episodes of *The Crocodile Hunter* and other shows, which have been shown in 142 countries. The shows and his larger-than-life Australian persona made Steve famous, and put the spotlight on environmental and animal conservation – especially education about reptiles.

Steve developed the family zoo, renaming it Australia Zoo in 1998, and it still functions as one of the most prestigious reptile parks in the world. In 2001 Steve was awarded the Centenary Medal by the Australian Government, and was also nominated for Australian of the Year in 2004.

Tragically, Steve died in 2006 when he was hit in the chest by a stingray's barb while snorkelling on the Great Barrier Reef. Terri and their children, Bindi and Robert, continue to promote the importance of animal conservation. Steve's name lives on through two critters too: in 1997 Steve had discovered a new species of turtle, which was later named Irwin's turtle (*Elseya irwini*), and a land snail was named after him in 2009 (*Crikey steveirwini*).

Steve, your infectious enthusiasm for nature educated many people about conservation and Australia's amazing wildlife.

We hope to be as passionate as you!

ILLUSTRATION BY SOFT SCIENCE

A HIGH FIVE TO

TAJ PABARI

FOR THINKING OF THE FUTURE

Fist bumps
to the young
entrepreneurs
who want to
change the world
and are out there
doing it.

TAJ PABARI

(1999–)

Taj Pabari is proof that age is just a number. The Indian-born Queenslander was just 11 when he created his own tech website and 15 when he began his company. While a school student might not fit most peoples' image of an inventor and tech entrepreneur, Taj is just that. His company, Fiftysix Creations, creates build-it-yourself computer tablets and coding kits for children and school students.

With the aim of introducing children as young as six to the world of computer science, Fiftysix Creations has been described as the 'Lego of the 21st century'. From his base in Logan, Queensland – a city less than one-tenth the size of Sydney or Melbourne – Taj has educated more than 100,000 children in how computer tablets work and how easy they are to build.

Taj advocates for teaching technical skills such as programming and coding, and 'soft' skills such as communication. As a younger boy he was shy about speaking in public, but learnt that it's no use having a great invention if you don't also have a way of telling people about it. He has consulted with the Queensland Curriculum and Assessment Authority on the skills today's young people will need in tomorrow's workplace, and his company runs Business Camp for student entrepreneurs aged 6 to 16. For every ticket sold, another ticket is given to a disadvantaged child.

Taj might just be the closest guy we have to Steve Jobs or Marvel's Iron Man Tony Stark, but he has one thing even Tony Stark doesn't: a Queensland Young Australian of the Year award.

Taj, you've shown us that we can make a difference to the world regardless of how old we are.

We want to change the world for the better too.

ILLUSTRATION BY DANIEL GRAY-BARNETT

A HIGH FIVE TO

TIM FLANNERY

FOR BEING AN EXPLORER EXTRAORDINAIRE

Let's follow
the path of
those who study
the past to
advocate for
the future.

TIM FLANNERY

(1956–)

As a boy, Tim Flannery would dive for fossils, looking for evidence of the marine megafauna that swam in our ancient seas. Inspired by his early experiences, Tim went on to study English, then geology, zoology and palaeontology. That might seem like quite a mix, but Tim has used his education in the most amazing ways.

He studied the evolution of kangaroos and named many new species, as well as helping in the discovery of Cretaceous period fossils that extended our knowledge of the Australian mammal fossil record by 80 million years. He explored remote areas of Papua New Guinea, finding many new mammal species in his travels. He has been a curator at Sydney's Australian Museum, a professor at the University of Adelaide and at Macquarie University, the director of the South Australian Museum, and a visiting chair at Harvard University in the United States of America.

More recently, the 2007 Australian of the Year has become known for fearlessly speaking up about the environment, sustainability and climate change. Tim challenges us all to think about how we use the resources we have and how we can preserve our natural heritage for future generations to appreciate and enjoy.

Tim, you're proof that if we're curious, adventurous and passionate, we can be anything we want to be.

We want to keep learning and discovering every day, just like you.

ILLUSTRATION BY CHRIS NIXON

A HIGH FIVE TO

TROYE SIVAN

FOR SHARING HIS TALENT AND HIS TRUTH

Click 'Follow', 'Like' and 'Subscribe' to all the talented teens who are forging amazing careers online and beyond.

TROYE SIVAN

(1995–)

By the age of 20 Troye Sivan Mellett had an international fan base of millions, a record contract and a debut album that went to number one on the iTunes chart in 24 countries. So how did a regular kid from a quiet suburb in Perth achieve global recognition? You guessed it – YouTube.

From a young age Troye had talent in spades, and he soon found the perfect platform to show off his passion for singing and performing. In 2007 he dipped his toe into the relatively new world of YouTube vlogging. He began to upload videos of himself singing cover versions of songs and daily updates on his life, loves and loathes. Followers were soon drawn to his honest and open nature, and in 2013 he came out as gay in a video on his channel.

His YouTube fame also landed him a life-changing record deal. His global success as a pop star can be credited to his outstanding talent and also to the fact he has never shied away from who he is. His songs, discussions and activism regularly reflect on sexuality and gender identity issues. For many teens and young adults, Troye has been a fixture for a large part of their lives, inspiring them to be honest about and proud of who they are.

While Troye may have shaped his stardom via video blogs, it's his music that has earned him staying power. With a critically acclaimed album under his belt and roles in films and theatre, Troye's career continues to go from strength to strength.

Troye, you're showing kids that it's possible to be true to themselves, be happy and smash career goals.

We will always 'Follow' you.

ILLUSTRATION BY BENJAMIN CONSTANTINE

A HIGH FIVE TO

VICTOR CHANG

FOR HIS ABSOLUTE BRILLIANCE

Give a hurrah
to those who
dedicate
themselves
to research
and medical
developments,
resulting in lives
being saved all
over the world.

VICTOR CHANG

(1936-1991)

Victor Peter Chang was born in Shanghai, China, to Australian-born parents. After high school he studied medicine at the University of Sydney, then trained and worked in various overseas hospitals before returning to Sydney and basing himself at St Vincent's Hospital.

His enthusiasm and dedication to cardiac research and medicine established St Vincent's as a leader in this field. Victor helped to develop an artificial heart valve and research the design for an artificial heart. He also founded the National Heart Transplant Program.

Victor's talent and dedication saved many lives and he strongly believed that the medical discovery and research his team pioneered were essential to helping even more people. Victor wanted to share skills and medical techniques with other hospitals, particularly those in South-East Asia. He nurtured these relationships and strengthened the bonds between Australia and other countries. He was named a Companion of the Order of Australia in 1986.

Victor died in 1991, the victim of a robbery gone wrong. His friends and patients have referred to him as kind, confidence-inspiring and humble. He was a beloved and brilliant surgeon and there was a national outpouring of sympathy for his wife and family after his tragically early death.

Victor, you were a pioneer in your field and your skill and dedication will never be forgotten!

We remember your legacy.

ILLUSTRATION BY LACHLAN CONN

A HIGH FIVE TO
VINCENT LINGIARI
FOR HIS COURAGEOUS CAMPAIGNING

Thank you to
the leaders in
our communities
who work for a
better future.

VINCENT LINGIARI

(1919–1988)

Vincent Lingiari grew up on a remote cattle station 600 kilometres south of Darwin in the Northern Territory. Vincent worked as a stockman along with many Aboriginal workers and became a highly respected Gurindji elder. When Vincent was promoted to head stockman, his salary was very small, especially compared to the wages non-Indigenous workers received.

In 1966, fed up with the pay injustices and appalling work conditions for Aboriginal people, Vincent led 200 of his people to walk off from their jobs in protest. The strike, which also called for his people's land to be returned to them, lasted many years and received media attention and support from non-Indigenous people as well as other Aboriginal communities suffering similar hardships. Vincent and other activists recorded the song 'Gurindji Blues' about their fight for equality, which sold 20,000 copies.

Finally in 1973 the federal government reached an agreement with the owner of the cattle station to lease some of the land to the Gurindji people, and the land was officially transferred to them two years later. This decision was an important influence on the events leading up to the implementation of the *Aboriginal Land Rights (Northern Territory) Act 1976*, and a milestone in Australian culture and the movement towards reconciliation.

Vincent, you showed with dignity how progress can be made by standing up for what is right.

We honour your memory and remember your struggle.

ILLUSTRATION BY GREGG DREISE

A HIGH FIVE TO

WALEED
ALY

FOR HIS AMAZINGLY
DIVERSE TALENTS

Here's to the people in the media who aren't afraid to make their voices heard when they see injustice and inequality.

WALEED ALY

(1978-)

Waleed Aly must be one of the busiest people in Australia. He holds degrees in chemical engineering and law, plus a doctorate, but you might know him best as a host on the hugely popular TV news program *The Project*. That's only the beginning! He also hosts the Radio National program 'The Minefield', writes regular articles in newspapers and lectures at the Monash University School of Social Sciences. Waleed is married to the author and academic Susan Carland, and they have two children. Plus he plays guitar in the rock band Robot Child. *Phew* . . .

While working in law, Waleed got his start in journalism by writing opinion pieces. As an Australian-born Muslim and a writer with an interest in precise language and consistent logic and ethics, he offered a point of view that was rarely given a platform in mainstream Australian media. Since then, he's written a book and numerous essays and articles.

In 2016 and 2017 he won the Gold Logie Award for Best Personality on Australian Television. He and producer Tom Whitty have been finalists for two Walkley Awards for excellence in journalism, for editorials on terrorism and preventing violence against women. Waleed is known for speaking out about issues that are important to him and his knack for engaging in thoughtful debate. On 'The Minefield', Waleed, his co-host and guests discuss tricky ethical questions, encouraging listeners to take an interest in a diverse range of topics and think deeply about the world.

Waleed, we love your passion for speaking out for what you believe in.

You inspire us to engage with the big questions life throws our way.

A HIGH FIVE TO

WEARY DUNLOP

FOR HIS BRAVERY AND TENACITY

Let's take a
moment to
honour those who
protect the weak
and defenceless,
especially in the
face of danger.

WEARY DUNLOP

(1907–1993)

Sir Ernest Edward 'Weary' Dunlop was born on 12 July 1907 and enjoyed a rambunctious childhood in north-eastern Victoria. He studied pharmacy and medicine at Melbourne University, where he was given the nickname 'Weary'. In November 1939 he enlisted in the Australian Army Medical Corps and served in Greece, Crete and North Africa.

Weary was in charge of an army hospital in Java, Indonesia, when the city fell to Japanese forces in 1942. Weary, his staff and patients were captured and transported to Singapore. After Weary was appointed Commander of the British and Australian prisoners, he and nearly 900 Allied men were moved to Konyu River Camp, Thailand, to work on the Thai–Burma Railway. The men were forced to endure gruelling physical labour in primitive conditions with little food. Many men perished and even more were scarred for life. Weary cared for the sick and dying, fought for better conditions for his men and often stood up to their captors at his own peril. Tales of Weary's selflessness and bravery during this time are legendary, and his actions earned him the lifelong loyalty of his men as well as the gratitude of a nation.

Despite the horrors he and his men experienced, Weary found it in himself to forgive their captors. He dedicated the rest of his life to the welfare of prisoners-of-war and their families, the causes of several health organisations and the fostering of diplomacy between Australia and Asia.

Weary, you displayed courage time and time again in the face of adversity. Not only were you a beacon of hope to your men and their fierce protector, you committed the ultimate act of bravery by forgiving.

We strive to be as compassionate as you.

ILLUSTRATION BY JAMES FOSDIKE

A HIGH FIVE TO
YOU!

Up high!
Down low!
To the side!
We're giving
ALL the kinds of
high five to the
boys and girls
who've found ace
Australian men to
celebrate inside
the pages of
this book.

ANDREW JOYNER

ANDREW WELDON

BENJAMIN CONSTANTINE

BRENTON McKENNA

BROLGA

CHRIS NIXON

DANIEL GRAY-BARNETT

DAVID HARDY

GREGG DREISE

HARRY SLAGHEKKE

JAMES FOSDIKE

JAMES GULLIVER HANCOCK

JAMES HART

JEREMY LORD

LACHLAN CONN

MATTHEW MARTIN

MULGA

RICHARD MORDEN

SOFT SCIENCE

TOHBY RIDDLE

TOM JELLETT

Acknowledgements

When we published *Shout Out to the Girls* earlier this year, a book shining light on the women of Australia who deserve to be recognised and celebrated, we were inundated with support. It was wonderful to be part of the incredibly important conversations and actions taking place everywhere to change our world for the better – to address inequalities, to make our society fairer for all, and to make sure everyone's voices are heard loud and clear.

And while men have historically had a far, far greater voice and representation in many spheres than women – which made it so very important for us to publish more stories about amazing women – we can't forget that we need to hear about positive male role models too. We want the next generation of young Australians to hear about the men who give us hope for the future, who inspire us in both everyday and extraordinary ways, whose actions exemplify what it means to be a top bloke in today's Australia.

So, thanks to all the requests we received for just such a book, the result is *High Five to the Boys* – a by no means comprehensive selection of just a few of the boys and men to whom we say, 'Mate, you rock.'

A double high five goes to those on our Penguin Random House team who eagerly put their hand up to write about men who make them proud. Thank you to Benjamin Fairclough, Catherine Hill, Catriona Murdie, Holly Toohey, Holly Willsher, Jessica Owen, Katrina Lehman, Kimberley Bennett, Laura Harris, Lindsey Hodder, Mary Verney, Patrick Mangan, Seamus McCarthy, Tom Langshaw, Tony Palmer, Victoria Stone and Zoe Walton.

We couldn't have created this book without the talented illustrators who brought our subjects to life so vividly – thank you to each and every one of you.

Another epic fist-bump needs to go to the book's incredible designer, Astred Hicks, who astounds us every day we work with her. We hope you love sharing this book with your son, Astred!

Finally, we know there's still a way to go in achieving equality, but we are grateful to the families, carers, teachers, mentors and friends who are helping the next generation to grow up believing in and working towards equality for all, and who champion the women and men who are helping us to get there.

A HIGH FIVE TO

THE SMITH FAMILY

FOR HELPING DISADVANTAGED
KIDS TO THRIVE AT SCHOOL

THE SMITH FAMILY

Founded 1922

All royalties from sales of *High Five to the Boys* will be donated to The Smith Family.

The Smith Family is Australia's leading children's education charity. It helps disadvantaged young Australians to succeed at school.

In Australia today there are 1.1 million children living in poverty.* The effects of family hardship go beyond a child's home life – it also affects their schooling. Without the things they need for school or access to additional outside-of-school support, disadvantaged children can fall further and further behind their classmates.

Not being able to keep up at school can lead to a child becoming disengaged from their learning. And without the skills or qualifications they need for a job, these young people will end up with poorer life outcomes overall.

However, investing in the education of a disadvantaged child delivers long-term positive benefits for them, their family and potentially generations to come. With Australians' support, The Smith Family is helping children in need to fit in at school, keep up with their peers and build aspirations for a better future for themselves.

*ACOSS Poverty Report, 2016

High fives and massive thankyous to The Smith Family for helping kids all across Australia get the most out of their education.

Readers, thank you for buying this book and supporting The Smith Family's wonderful work.

DESIGNER'S NOTE

The design celebrates the wide-ranging talents and interests of the men featured in this book and of all boys. Energetic patterns suggest possibility while the joyfully unrestrained colour palette embraces diversity and optimism. High-fiving hands reach out to acknowledge, support, salute and assist.